How To Interpret Handwriting

HUBERT DESENCLOS

CRESCENT BOOKS
NEW YORK • AVENEL, NEW JERSEY

CONTENTS

CLB 4401
© 1995 CLB Publishing, Godalming, Surrey, England
All rights reserved

This 1995 edition published by Crescent Books, distributed by Random House Value
Publishing, Inc.
40 Engelhard Avenue, Avenel, New Jersey 07001

Random House
New York • Toronto • London • Sydney • Auckland

A CIP catalog record for this book is available from the Library of Congress.

Printed and bound in Spain

ISBN 0-517-12171-9

8 7 6 5 4 3 2 1

ABOUT THE AUTHORS

Hubert Desenclos trained at the Société de Graphologie in Paris. He holds its Diploma, and also that of the Conservatoire Nationale des Arts et Métiers, Paris, where he studied occupational psychology and ergonomics. Hubert Desenclos has many years experience as a graphologist in Paris and London, and he currently teaches graphology in London.

Claire Desenclos is a novelist and journalist who has studied graphology. She assists with consultations and reports.

The authors would like to thank all those people whose handwriting appears in this book.

INTRODUCTION

Graphology is finding out a person's character through his or her handwriting. Just as a psychoanalyst searches for clues by listening to memories, a graphologist examines the marks on paper made by the writer's pen. Because these are formed by a lifetime of conscious and unconscious movements, they can reveal a great deal.

Graphology is a professional skill which is used increasingly all over the world and graphologists are able to assist psychologists, psychiatrists and marriage and vocational counsellors with character analyses, compatibility studies and aptitude assessment. It can also, if used with caution, help with job selection and conflict at work.

But it is not an abstruse subject which can be learned only in a college. You can teach yourself, and in the learning you will find out a surprising amount about yourself, the people you love, your friends, your job. All you need is a pencil, paper, a ruler (preferably a transparent one with ruled lines), and a magnifying glass.

Analysing handwriting is not the giving of definite meanings to letter forms, 't'-bars and so on. Rather, the tempo, fast or slow, even or uneven, and whether the writer manages to write the way he intended, are parts of the graphologist's basic investigation. They are clues to the deepest recesses of the writer's personality.

How the ideas and skills of graphology grew

The attempt to interpret handwriting has been going on ever since it was perceived that everyone's handwriting is different; Aristotle commented on this, and in the 17th century an Italian, Camillo Baldi, wrote a treatise on handwriting analysis. Writers including Goethe, Balzac, Edgar Allan Poe and Sir Walter Scott made intuitive speculations about it. This was during the first half of the 19th century, and a little later more disciplined researches into the subject began.

An Abbé Flandrin who taught at the great schools of Paris had the idea of studying his pupils' homework and relating their traits of character to their handwriting. He quickly attracted the active collaboration of his headmaster, the Abbé Michon, a brilliant and independent man who gave the decisive impulse to the idea of handwriting analysis (which he named 'graphology'). He wrote several books which are still interesting to read and developed a vocabulary of about 100 graphological features, eg slanted rightwards or leftwards, upright, connected, disconnected, wide, narrow, etc.

Among his students Michon had famous writers such as Georges Sand and Alexandre Dumas (the son), and also the man who was to be his graphological successor: Jean Crepieux-Jamin (1858–1940). First a clockmaker, then a dentist, Crepieux-Jamin's great skill was accuracy.

He took over Michon's list of features, added a hundred more and classified them into seven divisions: speed, pressure, direction, continuity, arrangement, form and dimension. He promoted one feature from Michon's list, Harmony, that is, good proportion and good taste with simplification, into the criterion of moral and intellectual superiority.

The list of graphological features still exists and is called *Jaminian features*, despite Michon's contribution. The *Michon-Jaminian features* (as they should be called) deserve respect, and the terminology is still valuable. This method was nevertheless purely based on observation and comparison between graphological features and the writer's character. As Michon, who was far from being dogmatic, constantly said, more research was needed.

For the next few decades many of the most fruitful ideas on graphology came from Germany, and they all dealt with the movement and the psychology behind the letter forms.

Around 1895 Wilhelm Preyer, a professor of psychophysiology, demonstrated that handwriting is generated by the brain, that the hand is only an instrument between the brain and pen. He collected the handwritings of people who had lost both their arms and had to write with their feet or mouth, and noticed that their handwriting kept the same characteristics. At about the same time the psychiatrist Georg Meyer began working out 'graphological structures', that is, the grouping of handwriting features which tend to appear together and express a certain psychological trait (syndrome), eg any of the categories in my chart (0–6, 10–16 etc.). Unfortunately Meyer died young and so had less influence than Ludwig Klages (1872–1956) who influenced graphology enormously for half a century, especially in Germany. Klages was a chemist who studied philosophy and then took up graphology. He was strongly influenced by the controversial German philosopher Nietzsche, who postulated the rule of the world by a race of supermen, and believed that the force of nature was more important than reason. Yet out of these extreme ideas Klages formed three theories useful to graphology: Rhythm, Form Level and the Guiding Image.

Rhythm: Klages contrasted 'measured' rhythm (soldiers marching) with 'natural' rhythm (waves, dancers). He thought that natural

Dumezil's handwriting.

Klages' handwriting

4

rhythm in writing (ie continuous alternation of moderate firmness and relaxation in up and down movement or modulation) was the expression of lively thought and feeling.

But a movement without relaxation of tension, however even, showed lack of rhythm (was unmodulated).

Klages, inspired by Nietzsche, contrasted the overcontrolled 'Apollonian' to the unrestrained 'Dionysian' style of life. He hated the theory of Harmony and replaced it with *Form Level*. This consisted of natural rhythm plus individuality of writing style. By this he meant the individuality arising spontaneously from the writer's nature and expressing him, conflicts, abilities and all, in a simplified, rhythmic and unique style.

People such as Beethoven are shown to have high Form Level, so certainly it reveals a kind of excellence; but, like *Harmony*, it must not be taken as the only standard. It is also dangerously subjective: the French were convinced Napoleon's Form Level was high, the Germans that it was not.

Beethoven's handwriting (high Form Level).

Napoleon's writing.

The *Guiding Image*, Klages' third theory, is that a writer unconsciously wishes his handwriting to have a certain appearance to fit his image of himself. This writer (bottom right), for instance, wants to give the impression of aesthetic niceness, but as it is not spontaneous it ends up as rather affected (the hyperconnections, the 'd's).

Contemporary with Klages were three other great European graphologists: Saudek, Hegar and Pulver.

Saudek was a Czech who emigrated to England in the 1920s, not as a refugee but because he found it restful, if a little boring. Saudek tried to give graphology a scientific basis. His most important theories were those of *Speed* and of *Standard Class*.

Speed: Saudek distinguished four *degrees of fluency* in handwriting.

1 *Stroke Impulse Level* (page 6), the lowest degree, is the one of a child learning to write; the child lifts his or her pen to write each separate stroke.

An example of lack of rhythm

Form Level very high: simplified, rhythmic, with room for irregularities. The writing of Dr R. Pophal, neurologist, psychiatrist and expert on graphological rhythm in relation to the nervous system.

Form Level below average: complicated and ostentatious, not spontaneously or naturally rhythmic.

Aesthetic but lacking spontaneity

2 *Letter Impulse leveL*, when the child lifts his or her pen after forming a letter before starting on the next one.

Some people able to write with word impulse keep the letter impulse level for aesthetical/psychological reasons, especially in calligraphic writing.

3 *Word Impulse Level*. Here the writer, child or adult, is able to write short words of two or three syllables without lifting his or her pen, but his or her attention is still focused on each word successively.

4 *Sentence Impulse Level*. The writer is able to concentrate on his or her message (thoughts). His or her letter formation is then simplified, the movement being cursive.

This classification of speed led to Saudek's other main theory, *Standard Class*, which is not much different from Klages' Form Level, except that it values speed and simplification more highly.

From Max Pulver (died 1952) came a very different point of view. He was the leader of the Swiss school of graphology, and lectured at the University of Zurich. Pulver did not like the value judgements implicit in Harmony, Form Level and Standard Class. He understood existential philosophy as well as psychoanalysis and analytic psychology, and he insisted that every graphological symptom had not one or two but several possible meanings, and that the meaning depended on the biological constitution and psychological complexes particular to each writer. This he called the *Existential Quality* and it is far more satisfactory because it judges people not in hierarchies of worth but according to their own potential.

Because Pulver understood philosophy and psychology he saw that the mind leaves marks of its unconscious symbolizing in handwriting, and this led him to introduce a fresh element into graphology – the *symbolism of space*.

Imagine, as Pulver did, that this blank page is your inner space and time. The 'me' who writes is a dot on the blank page. All round this 'me' and you can feel space – up, down, backward, forward; and time – the past, the future. The 'me', the dot, is here and now.

m
Stroke impulse level

cat
Letter impulse level

cat and dog
Word impulse level

They fight t and dog
Sentence impulse level

```
                    ME
                    HERE
                    NOW
PAST ◄──────────────•──────────────► FUTURE
```

Once the human mind has started symbolizing, it is apt to group sets of matching ideas together, like this:

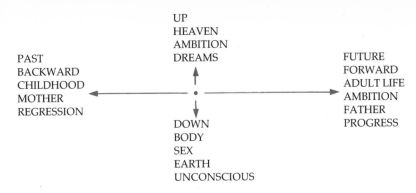

UP
HEAVEN
AMBITION
DREAMS

PAST
BACKWARD
CHILDHOOD
MOTHER
REGRESSION

FUTURE
FORWARD
ADULT LIFE
AMBITION
FATHER
PROGRESS

DOWN
BODY
SEX
EARTH
UNCONSCIOUS

Expressed in handwriting (see page 89 for graphological terms used), this is:

Forward and back:

1 *moon* 2 *moon* 3 *moon*

Leftward loops   Straight downstrokes   Cursive writing

1 The writing with leftward loops etc. shows unconscious attachment to the past, mother etc.
2 The straight forceful downstroke shows concern with me, here, now.
3 Cursive writing running toward the future.

Up and down:

Lower Zone: 1 Long, full loop clings to past and unconscious part of mind.

Upper Zone: 2 Thin, high stroke reaches up to ambition or mysticism.

Middle Zone: 3 Definite Middle Zone means a sense of self and reality.

The blank page can have other meanings. To Walter Hegar, a Jewish German research scientist who emigrated to Paris in the 1930s, it was a symbol of the external world. Strong pressure of the pen against the page, he thought, shows aggressiveness against the external world, whereas weak pressure shows acceptance or timidity. Out of this basic idea Hegar built a very useful theory. He was concerned not with the letter form but with the force underneath, the *basic stroke*, the movement and pressure of the pen. There were three elements in this basic stroke: 1) the pressure; 2) whether it was curved or straight; 3) whether it was fast or slow. He also considered whether it was clearcut or blurred at the edge, but this is less important since the use of Biros. A curved, rather slow movement with light pressure does not challenge the outside

The Lower Zone
Long full loop

The Upper Zone
Thin high stroke

The Middle Zone
Definite Middle Zone

world (light pressure) but instead tries to add something that is missing (curves, imagination). The elements of the basic stroke can be combined in several significant ways.

There has been a new upsurge in graphology all over the world. This goes with the recent growth of a wish for self-knowledge, and also with graphology's use in business. The French Société de Graphologie is still the academic centre but graphology is growing rapidly everywhere.

The Desenclos System

The system I have used in this book is one I have worked out after years of teaching and from my training in the Paris Société de Graphologie. It integrates the Michon-Jaminian features grouped according to movement and psychological syndrome. Saudek's, Hegar's and Pulver's ideas have all been very useful.

My system is basically a chart divided into six sections, one for each kind of writing movement and the psychology behind it. Both I and my students have found it fast and reliable.

In the interpretation I have followed the ideas of Freud, the post-Freudians and some other psychological and constitutional theories. There is no room in this book for a special section on how these theories can be used in graphology.

Harmony, Form Level, stages of development and the Three Qualities

Anyone who analyses handwriting has consciously or unconsciously to use some standard in judging it. Harmony and Form Level, already mentioned in this chapter, are still very much in vogue but make me feel uneasy.

The ability to write harmoniously goes with balance and discernment in the conduct of life. Someone who has high Form Level has realized the ability to express himself or herself with originality. But these standards, however useful, do not map the stages of development available to everyone. They do not take into account the fact that many people develop towards spontaneity and self-expression without specializing in extreme creativity.

The Harmony and Form Level theories are also severe on people who, because of the difficulties of their lives, will always have some tension, will always grip their pens too tightly and produce stiff and rhythmless handwriting, but who may have moved a long way in personal development from their starting point. The same applies to people whose individuality has hardly had a chance to form at all and who write conventionally or bolster themselves with artificiality.

Even with the stages of development taken into account, we still need some sort of standard that the development moves towards. I will call these the *Three Qualities*:

1 **Loving qualities** Sincerity, openmindedness, empathy, co-operation rather than competition and freedom from subservience. Shown in handwritings by: spontaneity, simplification, gentleness of movement without slackness. Some aggressiveness, if associated with warmth not coldness, is not incompatible with loving qualities.

2 **Discernment**. That is, with intellect and emotions not split from each other without necessarily going so far as the fine balance of harmony.

3 **Ability to form ideas from facts**. That is, some signs of a little creativity shown by freedom of movement in the handwriting, but this does not have to be artistic expression.

How to practise graphology

This book is a step-by-step method, using a chart to show how to analyse a handwriting.

You may, if you wish, choose the handwriting of someone you know and fill in the chart item by item. At the stage of filling in the chart there must be no attempt at interpreting what the meaning of the handwriting may be. Only when the chart is completed and the evidence of all the different kinds of writing movement has been collected will the book move on to interpretation. In each item there are examples of handwriting to make it clear what to look for.

In the second part, the interpretation, a worked example runs alongside the text from the beginning of the interpretation to the final portrait.

Graphology depends on 'eye training', that is, the ability to see if, for instance, the Middle Zone height is even or uneven. Like all skills, this comes with experience, but is fascinating from the first moment. A magnifying glass and ruler would be helpful.

The downstroke.

Basic vocabulary of graphology

Someone writing on paper produces *Letter Forms* which have a limited meaning unless they are traced back to the *Generative Movement* which has produced them.

The upstroke.

There are four basic movements in the act of writing (see examples):
1 The downstroke.
2 The upstroke.
3 The lateral stroke.
4 The circular stroke.
The stroke can be thick or thin, with or without *pressure*.

The lateral stroke.

The circular stroke.

The stroke between each downstroke is called a *Connective Stroke* (see example) and can be an upstroke or a lateral stroke. It can be inside the same letter or connect two letters.

There are three *zones* (see example):

1 The *Middle Zone* (MZ) Small letters etc. – the part between double lines in school exercise books.
2 The *Upper Zone* (UZ) Loops above this, 'i'-dots and 't'-bars.
3 The *Lower Zone* (LZ) Lower loops and projections.

About the handwriting you are analysing

You need to know the sex and approximate age of the writer. (If you know the writer well try not to let that prejudice you.)

Make sure the handwriting comes from a real letter and was not written specially, as this cramps the writer's style.

It should be a full page. Analyses based on less can be wrong.

It should be an original, as stroke movement and pressure are hard to judge on a photocopy.

The chart

The chart should be drawn and divided into six categories, for six different kinds of writing movement: 0–6 (speed); 10–16 (certainty of movement and flexibility); 20–28 (regularity); 30–36 (expansiveness); 40–46 (firmness); 50–54 (spontaneity). The chart is also divided into left and right. You mark on the right when the handwriting shows the movement in question (for example, speed) and on the left for its opposite (for example, slowness). Left and right are further divided into three columns to show the degree of movement – whether the speed is slight, moderate or marked.

LA to the left or RA to the right: to a slight degree.
LB to the left or RB to the right: to a moderate degree.
LC to the left or RC to the right: to a marked degree.

The chart has 42 items, not 54. The reader may wonder why a simpler numbering system (ie from 1 to 42) has not been adopted instead of leaving gaps between 6 and 10, 16 and 20 and so on. The reason for such a grouping is that each of these divisions deals with a particular aspect of the personality. It is consequently clearer to change the group of ten each time, so that one can refer to the '30s' or the '40s' group, etc.

A serious graphologist never judges a sign – a high 'i'-dot or an oversized or undersized part of a letter – in isolation. It is always related to the movement which produced it and successive items overlap within each category.

Connective strokes

NB: It is important to get the chart right, so work slowly and use your judgement. Don't worry if you make a mistake – preceding or following items will counterbalance and correct the error.

CHART		mkd LC	mod LB	sli LA	sli RA	mod RB	mkd RC		REF:
Emphasized first letters	0							0	Unemphasized first letters
Care of elaboration	1							1	Streamlined simplification
Left tendency: MZ	2							2	Right tendency: MZ
Left tending word endings	3							3	Right tending word endings
Left tendency: LZ	4							4	Right tendency: LZ
Left tendency: UZ	5							5	Right tendency: UZ
Interrupted movement	6							6	Connected movement
Narrowing or neat L margin	10							10	Widening L margin
Descending lines or words	11							11	Rising lines
Unmodulated pressure	12							12	Modulated pressure
Arcade connective forms	13							13	Garlandic connective forms
Slant stiffness	14							14	Slant flexibility
Close downstrokes	15							15	Wide-apart downstrokes
Close-packed letters	16							16	Wide-apart letters
Lines or words unparallel	20							20	Lines and words parallel
Irregular word spacing	21							21	Regular word spacing
Irregular margins	22							22	Regular margins
Irregular 'i'-dots	23							23	Regular 'i'-dots
Irregular slant	24							24	Regular slant
Irregular MZ height	25							25	Regular MZ height
Irregular LZ	26							26	Regular LZ
Disturbed pressure	27							27	Undisturbed pressure
Disturbed curves	28							28	Undisturbed curves
Lean MZ ovals	30							30	Full MZ ovals
Wide right margin	31							31	No right margin
Limited movement (any zone)	32							32	Animated movement (any zone)
Short LZ	33							33	Long LZ
Lean LZ	34							34	Full LZ
Clear interlines	35							35	Overlapping projections
Low 'i'-dots	36							36	High 'i'-dots
Wide space between words	40							40	Narrow space between words
Lines not straight	41							41	Lines straight
Downstroke not straight	42							42	Downstrokes straight
Weak pressure	43							43	Strong pressure
Soft or unfinished endings	44							44	Stress on ending strokes
Weak or omitted 't'-bars	45							45	Stressed 't'-bars/cross-strokes
Soft rounded forms	46							46	Angular forms
Inadequate spacing	50							50	Adequate spacing
Letters out of proportion	51							51	Letters in proportion
Slow from any cause (0–16L)	52							52	Natural and fast (0–16R)
Conventional forms	53							53	Individual forms
Stiffness or monotony	54							54	Natural rhythm

UZ = Upper zone   MZ = Middle zone   LZ = Lower zone

CATEGORY ONE
0–6 SPEED THROUGH SIMPLIFICATION

Speed in the writing movement can result from simplification, certainty, flexibility or all three. Category One (0–6) deals with the simplification that has developed to allow the writing movement to be rapid, or the care and elaboration that slows down movement.

To take care and elaboration first: these are signs that the writer is less interested in conveying a thought as fast as possible than in showing by his handwriting what kind of person he is. This delays the speed and can be seen in the following ways: when the first letter is too much emphasized; when the letter forms are complicated; when the writing movement in all zones and in word endings keeps turning back towards the left, and when the letters are not connected. All these should be marked on the left side of the chart.

Simplifications that help the speed are known as the mental factors of speed (certainty and flexibility are called the temperamental factors of speed and are dealt with in Category Two). These 'mental' simplifications can be seen in the following ways: when the first letter, capital or not, fits well with the rest of the word; when the letter forms have been simplified in clever ways (*the letters in example A are both simple forms, but whereas three lifts of the pen were necessary for the first letter, the second was formed in a single movement*). The writing movement can be simplified still further by clever connections between letters, and by joining 'i'-dots and 't'-bars to the following letters. Two more signs of simplification to help speed are when the writing movement in all zones and in word endings is towards the right, and when there are flowing or even flying and almost unseen 'aerial connections' between the letters. All these should be marked on the right side of the chart except the 'unseen connections', which will need crosses.

The seven items within Category One are:
0 Emphasis on first letter
1 Simplification of forms
2 Direction of movement in the Middle Zone
3 Direction of movement in word endings
4 Direction of movement in the Lower Zone
5 Direction of movement in the Upper Zone
6 Continuity

		mkd	mod	sli	sli	mod	mkd		
		LC	LB	LA	RA	RB	RC		
Emphasized first letters	0							0	Unemphasized first letters
Care or elaboration	1							1	Streamlined simplification
Left tendency: MZ	2							2	Right tendency: MZ
Left-tending word endings	3							3	Right tending word endings
Left tendency: LZ	4							4	Right tendency: LZ
Left tendency: UZ	5							5	Right tendency: UZ
Interrupted movement	6							6	Connected movement

Item 0 Emphasis On First Letter
Emphasized first letters or Unemphasized first letters

The first letter of a word, especially if it is a capital, throws some light on the writer's concern with his self-image.

Someone whose self-image is important to him will exaggerate the necessary difference between capitals and non-capitals and even emphasize the non-capital first letter of a word. He will also take some care with the personal pronoun 'I'. All these features should be marked on the left side of the chart.

Someone whose concern about his self-image is a secondary matter will be freer to convey his message in a sentence impulse (see Introduction on page 4). In this case the capital letters will be of modest size and often connected to the rest of the word, still more so the non-capital first letter. The personal pronoun 'I' will not be emphasized. All these features should be marked on the right side of the chart.

What to look for
Emphasized first letter and 'I' – left side of chart:
Ornamentation, excessive width or height, disconnection.

Item 0

Ornamentation

mkd	mod	sli	sli	mod	mkd
LC	LB	LA	RA	RB	RC
	●				

Emphasized personal pronoun 'I'

mkd	mod	sli	sli	mod	mkd
LC	LB	LA	RA	RB	RC
		●			

Oversized (height) initial letter, capitals and non capitals

mkd	mod	sli	sli	mod	mkd
LC	LB	LA	RA	RB	RC
	●				

Oversized (width) initial capitals

mkd	mod	sli	sli	mod	mkd
LC	LB	LA	RA	RB	RC
●					

Disconnected first letter, capitals and non capitals

mkd	mod	sli	sli	mod	mkd
LC	LB	LA	RA	RB	RC
	●				

First letters and 'I' without emphasis – right side of chart:
Simplified capitals, often joined to the rest of the word.

mkd	mod	sli	sli	mod	mkd
LC	LB	LA	RA	RB	RC
					●

Item 1 Simplification of Forms
Care or elaboration or Streamlined simplification

Some writers take unnecessary care about the appearance of their handwriting and produce painstaking or elaborate forms which are factors of slowness and should be marked on the left of the chart.

Those writing with sentence impulse simplify their forms by letting them flow to the right in a streamlined way so that the ends of words, syllables and some letters such as 'm' and 'n' decrease rhythmically in height. They simplify the forms further by clever connections, that is by finding economical, almost shorthand ways of combining strokes. Such features should be marked on the right side of the chart.

What to look for
Careful or elaborate letter formation – left side of chart:
Painstaking care, artificial, elaborate or very conventional forms, ends of words increasing in height.*

Painstaking, aiming at perfect copybook forms and even size

Item 1

mkd	mod	sli	sli	mod	mkd
LC	LB	LA	RA	RB	RC
●					

Complicated, finicky, artificial

mkd	mod	sli	sli	mod	mkd
LC	LB	LA	RA	RB	RC
●					

* Copybook or conventional forms that are not painstaking, finicky or elaborate should be marked on the middle line.

14

Conventional and elaborate

[handwriting sample: "School will affect our ... together. Lots of you ll be thinking of you you ll spend part of you close friends . Love"]

mkd	mod	sli	sli	mod	mkd
LC	LB	LA	RA	RB	RC
●					

Last letters of words increasing in height (especially 'mothers')

[handwriting sample: "Next week. Lewis' My mother's you fall"]

mkd	mod	sli	sli	mod	mkd
LC	LB	LA	RA	RB	RC
●					

Streamlined simplification – right side of chart:

Streamlined forms with word endings decreasing in height, clever simplifications and neglect of details.

Clever simplifications: 'i'-dot of 'his' joined to next letter, 't'-bar of 'writing' joined to next letter and other 'i'-dots dashed

[handwriting sample: "seen his writing before."]

mkd	mod	sli	sli	mod	mkd
LC	LB	LA	RA	RB	RC
					●

Clever simplifications and details neglected: two 't' bars omitted, one 'i'-dot joined to next letter, and a simplified capital 'e'

[handwriting sample: "articles on Educatio"]

mkd	mod	sli	sli	mod	mkd
LC	LB	LA	RA	RB	RC
					●

Word endings reduced in height: eg, 'n' and 'm'

[handwriting sample: "thing at a time,"]

mkd	mod	sli	sli	mod	mkd
LC	LB	LA	RA	RB	RC
					●

Item 2 Direction of Movement in the Middle Zone
Left tendency in Middle Zone or Right tendency in Middle Zone

The natural flow of the writing movement is rightwards, so any unnecessary movements of the pen towards the left will slow the pace. Some leftward movement is, of course, unavoidable if the letters are to be properly formed, but certain handwritings are characterized by 'left-tending' or 'regressive' movements. In the Middle Zone these can be seen when 'o' and 'a' are too tightly knotted, when the stems of the 'm' and 'n' have unnecessary loops, or when any unnecessary curves or triangles are formed. All such features should be marked on the left side of the chart.

Writers with the sentence impulse will bother very little with the leftward letter formation and their writing movement will be 'right-tending' or 'progressive'. There will be no superfluous strokes, the ovals of 'o' and 'a' will be open on top and the stems of 'm', 'n' and other letters may be open. All such features should be marked on the right side of the chart.

What to look for
Left tendency in MZ – left side of chart:
Ovals knotted, looped connections, leftward angles or curves.

Both 'a' and 'g' over-knotted

Item 2

mkd	mod	sli	sli	mod	mkd
LC	LB	LA	RA	RB	RC
●					

Looped connection in the 'n' of 'strange' and closed vowel 'a'

mkd	mod	sli	sli	mod	mkd
LC	LB	LA	RA	RB	RC
	●				

Oval of 'o' joined twice but rest of the word not left-tending

mkd	mod	sli	sli	mod	mkd
LC	LB	LA	RA	RB	RC
	X	●	X		

Regressive triangular connective forms

mkd	mod	sli	sli	mod	mkd
LC	LB	LA	RA	RB	RC
●					

Right tendency in MZ – right side of chart:
Ovals open on top, stems of 'm' and 'n' open, no superfluous loops or covering strokes, simplified.

Ovals open at the top of 'o' and 'a'. Fairly simplified and fast

mkd	mod	sli	sli	mod	mkd
LC	LB	LA	RA	RB	RC
				●	

'm' and 'n' look alike because of simplified fast movement in 'minimum',
but still legible

[handwriting sample]

mkd	mod	sli	sli	mod	mkd
LC	LB	LA	RA	RB	RC
					●

Simplified and fast with
no covering strokes

[handwriting sample]

mkd	mod	sli	sli	mod	mkd
LC	LB	LA	RA	RB	RC
				●	

Item 3 Direction of Movement in Word Endings
Left tendency in word endings or Right tendency in word endings

Some writers lift the pen before they have finished the word,
which results in a short ending stroke or even an unfinished last
letter. Others turn the ending stroke in a backward, that is
leftward, direction. Both these impede the speed and should be
marked on the left side of the chart.

People who are eager to get the message across as fast as possible,
that is with sentence impulse, tend to direct the ending stroke of
the word towards the next word. At the end of the line they
sometimes direct the ending stroke towards the next line. These
are signs of speed and should be marked on the right side of the
chart.

What to look for
Left tendency in word endings – left side of chart:
Ending stroke stopped short, hooked, centripetal, turned left.

Ends of words stopped short ('have', 'let', 'me')

Item 3

[handwriting sample]

mkd	mod	sli	sli	mod	mkd
LC	LB	LA	RA	RB	RC
		●			

Restrained movement but final
stroke of 'manage' hooks
upwards to the left

[handwriting sample: manage]

mkd	mod	sli	sli	mod	mkd
LC	LB	LA	RA	RB	RC
X	●	X			

Final 'n' in 'commun' has short centripetal ending. Final 'n' in 'decision'
ends with a hook to the left

[handwriting sample: commun decision]

mkd	mod	sli	sli	mod	mkd
LC	LB	LA	RA	RB	RC
X	●	X			

Ending strokes turned up to the left

my return).
together that

mkd	mod	sli	sli	mod	mkd
LC	LB	LA	RA	RB	RC
●					

Right tendency in word endings – right side of chart:
Ending stroke directed towards next word or even next line.

Ending stroke of each word is directed to the right

The latest on the house move

mkd	mod	sli	sli	mod	mkd
LC	LB	LA	RA	RB	RC
					●

Ending stroke of each word is directed to the right and the last stroke in each line is directed downwards to next line

The others are the present

mkd	mod	sli	sli	mod	mkd
LC	LB	LA	RA	RB	RC
			●		

Item 4 Direction of Movement in the Lower Zone
Left tendency in Lower Zone or Right tendency in Lower Zone

There are many handwritings, especially those of women, in which the left-tending movement is only in the Lower Zone and is done in a graceful, curved way: see example A. Sometimes however, the left-tending movement in the Lower Zone is angular, triangular or reversed and complicated. In all these cases the mark should be on the left side of the chart.

The right-tending movement in the Lower Zone can take any of these three forms: a slender rounded loop which connects to the next letter; an unlooped projection with some concavity to the right; or, and this is the most extreme, an unlooped projection which is connected to the next letter in an anticlockwise movement instead of a loop (example below). All these should be marked on the right side of the chart.

What to look for
Left tendency in LZ – left side of chart:
Graceful unlooped leftward curve, inflated loop, triangle or complicated reversed forms

18

Graceful leftward curves, not joined to next letter

my handwriting being

mkd	mod	sli	sli	mod	mkd
LC	LB	LA	RA	RB	RC
	●				

Fat, leftward curves

Je garde Aoïgue me donne , fab

mkd	mod	sli	sli	mod	mkd
LC	LB	LA	RA	RB	RC
●					

Leftward, sharp triangle

actually

mkd	mod	sli	sli	mod	mkd
LC	LB	LA	RA	RB	RC
●					

Complicated reversed LZ in 'J'

Jeff.

mkd	mod	sli	sli	mod	mkd
LC	LB	LA	RA	RB	RC
✗	●	✗			

Right tendency in the LZ – right side of chart:

Slender loop connecting to next letter, unlooped projection with some concavity to the right, or anticlockwise stroke connecting unlooped projection.

The LZ of each word bends slightly to the right

feel free

mkd	mod	sli	sli	mod	mkd
LC	LB	LA	RA	RB	RC
				●	

The slender loop of the LZ connects to the next letter

Monday midnight

mkd	mod	sli	sli	mod	mkd
LC	LB	LA	RA	RB	RC
				●	

A simple stroke connects the unlooped LZ to the next MZ letter

yan

mkd	mod	sli	sli	mod	mkd
LC	LB	LA	RA	RB	RC
					●

Item 5 Direction of Movement in the Upper Zone
Left tendency in Upper Zone or Right tendency in Upper Zone

Left-tending movement can show in the Upper Zone in inflated loops, unnecessary loops or sometimes in graceful regressive curves like example A. Also in the Upper Zone are the 'i'-dots and 't'-bars which, as they are separate from the rest of the word and usually formed without conscious thought, can reveal a great deal about the writing movement. When 'i'-dots are left-tending they are placed on the left of the stem, or are replaced by circles. Left-tending 't'-bars can be completely on the left of the stem, or they can start from the left of the stem and form a cross, a lasso or a triangle. All these should be marked on the left side of the chart.

Slender Upper Zone loops, and 'i'-dots and 't'-bars propelled forwards of the stem, directed downwards towards the next letter or even connected to it, and sometimes omitted altogether, should be marked on the right side of the chart.

What to look for
Left tendency in UZ – left side of chart:

Inflated or unnecessary loop, graceful regressive curve, 'i'-dots and 't'-bars to left of stem, circular 'i'-dots, 't'-bar in cross, lasso or triangle.

Item 5

UZ loops inflated, especially the 's' of 'seeing' which should be in MZ

mkd	mod	sli	sli	mod	mkd
LC	LB	LA	RA	RB	RC
	●				

't'-bar to left of stem. Additional leftward loops on 't' and 'd'

mkd	mod	sli	sli	mod	mkd
LC	LB	LA	RA	RB	RC
●					

Lyrical 'd'

mkd	mod	sli	sli	mod	mkd
LC	LB	LA	RA	RB	RC
		●			

Circular 'i'-dots to the left of stem, but UZ loops short and stylized

mkd	mod	sli	sli	mod	mkd
LC	LB	LA	RA	RB	RC
X		●	X		

't'-bar complicated, to the left of stem

mkd	mod	sli	sli	mod	mkd
LC	LB	LA	RA	RB	RC
●					

Right tendency in UZ – right side of chart:

Loops slender or no loops, 'i'-dots and 't'-bars to right of stem, sometimes in clever connection with next letter and sometimes omitted.

Simplified UZ with 'i'-dots and 't'-bars connected to following letters

mkd	mod	sli	sli	mod	mkd
LC	LB	LA	RA	RB	RC
			X	●	X

20

'␣t'-bars to the right of stem, one of
them continuing towards the
right in a long stroke. All 'i'-dots,
except one, to the right

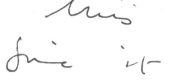

mkd	mod	sli	sli	mod	mkd
LC	LB	LA	RA	RB	RC
		X		●	X

Simplified UZ. No 't'-bar in 'articles' and dashed 'i' joined to next letter,
'i'-dot in 'mine' dashed and far to the right

mkd	mod	sli	sli	mod	mkd
LC	LB	LA	RA	RB	RC
					●

'i'-dot omitted in simplified writing

mkd	mod	sli	sli	mod	mkd
LC	LB	LA	RA	RB	RC
			●		

Item 6 Continuity
Interrupted movement or Connected movement

When the letters are connected to each other within a word this is a
sign of speed, but when each letter is disconnected from the one
before it and the one following, the writer has obviously lifted the
pen each time and so slowed down the writing. The movement is
even slower when the letters are perfectly formed or stylized, and
some writers even go back and make 'false connections'
afterwards. All these should be marked on the left side of the chart.

There is, however, a different kind of disconnected writing that is
caused not by slow but by fast, rhythmical movement where the
writer's pen begins a rightward continuing stroke and then leaps
between one letter and the next without touching the paper. This is
called 'aerial continuity' and goes with 0–5R, especially 1R. It
should be marked in Item 6 with a cross on the left side and one on
the right, perhaps quite far to the right. An example of this feature
is shown below.

When the letters are connected to each other within the word the
writer has not lifted the pen and so the movement is faster. Some
connectedness can be a fairly solid movement when it is along the
baseline. However, if the connective strokes are cursive and
possibly trizonal as well (that is, flowing easily from zone to zone),
this implies a faster movement. Some writers even connect one
word to the next in what are called hyperconnections. All these are

signs of continuity which help the speed and are marked on the right side of the chart.

What to look for

Interrupted movement – left side of chart:

No connection between printed, stylized or inflated letters. False connections.

Almost no connections between the print-like letters. The 'm' of 'me' and 'h' of 'has' are formed by centripetal (downward) movements which are far from continuous

come back from a
tells me he has

mkd	mod	sli	sli	mod	mkd
LC	LB	LA	RA	RB	RC
●					

No connection between the LZ 'p' and the following 'o' or between 'y' and the following 'o'

to inform you,

mkd	mod	sli	sli	mod	mkd
LC	LB	LA	RA	RB	RC
	X	●		X	

Interruption through stylization

didn't survive their

mkd	mod	sli	sli	mod	mkd
LC	LB	LA	RA	RB	RC
●					

False connections: 'n' in 'control' formed in two movements; no true connection between the 'o' and 'n' in 'one'

control one

mkd	mod	sli	sli	mod	mkd
LC	LB	LA	RA	RB	RC
●					

Connected movement – right side of chart:

Connection on baseline; aerial connections; cursive and trizonal connections; hyperconnections.

Continuous connection, always on base of MZ and solid in comparison with the rest of the letters

now we will

mkd	mod	sli	sli	mod	mkd
LC	LB	LA	RA	RB	RC
				●	

The 't'-bar of 'handwriting' joins the 'i'. In 'this' the 'i'-dot is dashed and joins the 's'. Aerial continuity is also evident

handwriting in this

mkd	mod	sli	sli	mod	mkd
LC	LB	LA	RA	RB	RC
				●	

Breaks in words occur in rational groups; eg 'wri' leaves room for 'i'-dot before 'ting' in 'writing'. Aerial continuity is also evident

mkd	mod	sli	sli	mod	mkd
LC	LB	LA	RA	RB	RC
			●		

The 'y' of 'yourself' is joined in a continuing stroke to the following 'o'. Such connections are less common than might be expected

mkd	mod	sli	sli	mod	mkd
LC	LB	LA	RA	RB	RC
				●	

Disconnection with aerial continuity

mkd	mod	sli	sli	mod	mkd
LC	LB	LA	RA	RB	RC
		X	●	X	

Easy movement between all three zones with flowing continuity and trizonal connection

mkd	mod	sli	sli	mod	mkd
LC	LB	LA	RA	RB	RC
					●

Hyperconnections between words

mkd	mod	sli	sli	mod	mkd
LC	LB	LA	RA	RB	RC
					●

CATEGORY TWO
10–16 SPEED FROM CERTAINTY OF MOVEMENT AND FLEXIBILITY

This category analyses the speed of the handwriting from the point of view of certainty versus hesitancy of movement and flexibility versus stiffness. These characteristics depend more on temperamental disposition than on mental organization of the writing movement.

Hesitancy of the stroke movement can be seen in faltering lines, words, letters or strokes and also in the narrowness of the left margin and between strokes and letters. Stiffness is revealed by lack of variability in slant or modulation in pressure, and by an extremely neat left margin. All these features should be marked on the left side of the chart.

Certainty of movement produces a widening left margin and rising straight lines. Flexibility results in modulated and moderate pressure, garlandic connective forms, slant flexibility and width in general. All these features should be marked on the right side of the chart.

The seven items covered in Category Two are:

10 Direction of margins
11 Direction of lines
12 Pressure modulation
13 Connective forms

14 Slant flexibility
15 Width between downstrokes
16 Width between letters

		mkd	mod	sli	sli	mod	mkd		
		LC	LB	LA	RA	RB	RC		
Narrowing or neat L margin	10							10	Widening L margin
Descending lines or words	11							11	Rising lines
Unmodulated pressure	12							12	Modulated pressure
Arcade connective forms	13							13	Garlandic connective forms
Slant stiffness	14							14	Slant flexibility
Close downstrokes	15							15	Wide-apart downstrokes
Close-packed letters	16							16	Wide-apart letters

Item 10 Direction of Margins
Narrowing or neat left margin or Widening left margin

A careful writer who likes neatness or respects convention will not start a new line without making sure that he has put his pen at the correct place for the margin. This of course slows down the movement. Other writers start each successive line more to the left because they unconsciously restrain their movements. This results in a narrowing of the left margin, either right to the bottom of the page or renewed in each successive paragraph. All such features slow down the movement of the writing and should be marked on the left of the chart.

Some writers are so impatient to get their message across that they unconsciously start each successive line more to the right. This produces a widening margin either from the top to the bottom of the page or within each paragraph. This is a factor of speed and should be marked on the right side of the chart.

What to look for
Neat or narrowing left margin – left side of chart:
Left margin perfectly neat and vertical. Left margin diminishing in width, can be in successive paragraphs.

Left margin neat and vertical

Progressively narrowing margin,
paragraph by paragraph

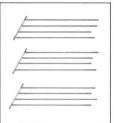

mkd	mod	sli	sli	mod	mkd
LC	LB	LA	RA	RB	RC
●					

mkd	mod	sli	sli	mod	mkd
LC	LB	LA	RA	RB	RC
	●				

Widening left margin – right side of chart:

Whole margin widening or in successive paragraphs. Can be
regular or not.

Margin widening in fairly regular
line

Margin progressively
widening paragraph by
paragraph (excluding
indentations). Fairly regular

Margin rapidly widening
in very regular line

mkd	mod	sli	sli	mod	mkd
LC	LB	LA	RA	RB	RC
				●	

mkd	mod	sli	sli	mod	mkd
LC	LB	LA	RA	RB	RC
				●	

mkd	mod	sli	sli	mod	mkd
LC	LB	LA	RA	RB	RC
					●

Item 11 Direction of Lines
Descending lines or words or Rising lines

When lines or words within the line descend below the horizontal
this is the result of a faltering movement which slows down the
speed and should be marked on the left side of the chart.

When lines rise consistently and are straight, this is a sign of
certainty of movement, and the mark should be on the right of the
chart.

What to look for
Descending lines or words – left side of chart:
Lines descending in even or uneven way, words within lines descending in steps.

Words descending in steps

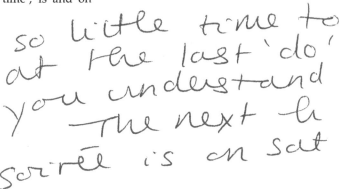

mkd	mod	sli	sli	mod	mkd
LC	LB	LA	RA	RB	RC
●					

Descending lines parallel and fairly even but downward slant increases towards bottom of page

Rising lines – right side of chart:
Straight rising lines, or lines rising but uneven, with rising words.

Lines rising but not straight. Words rising within the lines; eg, 'little' and 'time', 'is' and 'on'

mkd	mod	sli	sli	mod	mkd
LC	LB	LA	RA	RB	RC
	●				

mkd	mod	sli	sli	mod	mkd
LC	LB	LA	RA	RB	RC
				●	

Rising straight lines

mkd	mod	sli	sli	mod	mkd
LC	LB	LA	RA	RB	RC
					●

Item 12 Pressure Modulation
Unmodulated pressure or Modulated pressure

The modulation between pressure and release in the writing movement shows in the thickness and thinness of the strokes. When the downstroke and upstroke are of the same thickness this is a sign that the pressure is unmodulated and without the rhythm of pressure and release. Unmodulated pressure can be either all heavy, in which case both upstroke and downstroke are thick, or all light when both are thin, but in both cases the writing movement is restrained. This is a sign of slowness, so the mark should be on the left side of the chart.

When the pressure is well-modulated in a rhythmical way the downstroke will be moderately thick but well-shaped and the upstroke thinner but not abruptly so. This modulation allows the writing movement to be flexible and fast so it is marked on the right side of the chart.

A magnifying glass is necessary as the strokes have to be examined thoroughly, especially as modern pens are not usually flexible enough to make very distinctive marks. It is also helpful to turn the page over and feel the back for the welts made by the pressure.

What to look for
Unmodulated pressure – left side of chart:
Upstroke and downstroke same thickness in light writing or in heavy writing.

Lack of pressure on both upstroke and downstroke

grown up I work in the

mkd	mod	sli	sli	mod	mkd
LC	LB	LA	RA	RB	RC
	●				

Heavy pressure on both upstroke and downstroke; no modulation

but I couldn't

mkd	mod	sli	sli	mod	mkd
LC	LB	LA	RA	RB	RC
	●				

Modulated pressure – right side of chart:
Downstroke thicker than upstroke but transition not abrupt.

Lively modulation between upstroke and downstroke. (The writing of the artist Joan Miró)

de faire renouveller

mkd	mod	sli	sli	mod	mkd
LC	LB	LA	RA	RB	RC
				●	

Item 13 Connective Forms
Arcade connective forms or Garlandic connective forms

These join one stroke to the next inside the letters as well as between letters. The two kinds of connective form studied in this item are the 'arcade' which is like an arch, and the 'garland' which is like a garland (see examples on following pages). Angle and thread, which are the two other connective forms, are dealt with in Item 46 on page 65.

Arch

Garland

The arcade connective form joins the downstrokes of 'm' and 'n' in the copybook model learned at school, and some adult writers not only stick to it, but accentuate the arch and the parallelism of the downstrokes and use it in several other letters. This takes time to write and so should be marked on the left side of the chart.

Simplified and casual arcades can be marked close to the middle line even in RZ when very simplified and streamlined.

Garlandic connective forms proceed from an anti-clockwise movement and are more compatible with a rhythmic flexible movement. They are consequently a factor of speed, provided they are done spontaneously, and should be marked on the right side of the chart. If they are square or artificial they should be marked near the middle of the chart.

What to look for
Arcade connective forms – left side of chart:
Arcades can be accentuated with the arch very clear or simplified or streamlined.

Item 13

Extreme arcades with covering strokes occasionally increasing in height

immediate

mkd	mod	sli	sli	mod	mkd
LC	LB	LA	RA	RB	RC
●					

Streamlined, simplified arcades

hoping

television   eventual

mkd	mod	sli	sli	mod	mkd
LC	LB	LA	RA	RB	RC
				●	

Simplified arcade   *concerned*

mkd	mod	sli	sli	mod	mkd
LC	LB	LA	RA	RB	RC
		●			

Garlandic connective forms – right side of chart:
Garlands can be spontaneous, looped, threadlike, artificial, square, rounded or angular.

Spontaneous, rapid garlands, eg 'm' in 'meantime'

in the mean

mkd	mod	sli	sli	mod	mkd
LC	LB	LA	RA	RB	RC
					●

Looped garlands which avoid all angles and increase speed of writing, eg the first 'r' in 'returned'. In spite of movement to the left there are also covering strokes and tendency to square garlands

Please send returned

mkd	mod	sli	sli	mod	mkd
LC	LB	LA	RA	RB	RC
				●	

Threadlike garland; 'm' and 'n' in 'company'

company we

mkd	mod	sli	sli	mod	mkd
LC	LB	LA	RA	RB	RC
					●

Angular garland; 'm' in 'time' and 'them'	*time with them*	mkd	mod	sli	sli	mod	mkd
		LC	LB	LA	RA	RB	RC
						●	

Item 14 Slant Flexibility
Slant stiffness or Slant flexibility

The common assumption that rightward slant is a factor of speed and leftward slant of slowness must be taken with reserve. What is important in this instance is the flexibility versus the stiffness of the up and down movement.

When the downstrokes are parallel in a stiff or monotonous way, even with a rightward slant, the speed is hindered and the chart should be marked on the left.

There are two main kinds of flexibility in slant which contribute to fast writing: either the slant is slightly to the right and the forms semi-rounded, or the writing is rather upright with wide, rounded forms and thready garlands. Both these should be marked on the right side of the chart.

What to look for
Slant stiffness – left side of chart:
Stiff rightward or leftward slant, or stiff and upright.

Item 14

Stiff rightward slant, excessively regular

things very late. taking his O levels has a bad back

mkd	mod	sli	sli	mod	mkd
LC	LB	LA	RA	RB	RC
	●				

Stiff leftward slant

Politically, things all know about the recession

mkd	mod	sli	sli	mod	mkd
LC	LB	LA	RA	RB	RC
	●				

Upright and stiff   *money.*

mkd	mod	sli	sli	mod	mkd
LC	LB	LA	RA	RB	RC
	●				

Slant flexibility – right side of chart:
Slant slightly to right with semi-rounded forms, or rather upright with wide, rounded forms and thready garlands.

Slight rightward slant, increasing towards end of line. Modulated, medium pressure

phone so I thought

mkd	mod	sli	sli	mod	mkd
LC	LB	LA	RA	RB	RC
				●	

Rather upright letters with wide, rounded forms and thready tendency

indeed.

mkd	mod	sli	sli	mod	mkd
LC	LB	LA	RA	RB	RC
				●	

Item 15 Width Between Downstrokes
Close downstrokes or Wide-apart downstrokes

When a writer places downstrokes close together this is a restrained movement which slows down the speed, whereas downstrokes far apart are the sign of a loose or confident movement which is likely to be fast as well.

The best way to judge the width between downstrokes is to examine the 'u' and 'n' in the handwriting. If they are higher than they are wide the downstrokes are close together and the movement is slow. This should be marked on the left side of the chart. If the 'n' and 'u' are wider than they are high the downstrokes are far apart and the movement is likely to be reasonably fast. This should be marked on the right side.

What to look for
Close downstrokes – left side of chart:
Downstrokes close together in 'n' and 'u'.

Item 15

mkd	mod	sli	sli	mod	mkd
LC	LB	LA	RA	RB	RC
●					

Letters 'n', 'w' and 'u' higher than they are wide

present we pronounce

Wide-apart downstrokes – right side of chart:
Downstrokes far apart in 'n' and 'u'.

Fast, flexible handwriting. The downstrokes of 'n', 'u', 'h' and 'y' are wide apart, making the MZ part of the letters wider than they are high

ing the holiday

mkd	mod	sli	sli	mod	mkd
LC	LB	LA	RA	RB	RC
					●

Item 16 Width Between Letters
Close-packed letters or Wide-apart letters

Some writers pack their wide and well-rounded letters close together with no room for connective strokes. In others restrained movement results in narrowness between letters as well as between downstrokes. In both cases this narrowness between letters is a sign of slowness and the mark should be on the left side of the chart.

A more fluent movement which tends to fly from one letter to the next results in some width between letters. These are generally connected but can be linked by aerial movement (see Item 6 on page 21). When the letters are wide apart the mark should be on the right of the chart.

What to look for
Close-packed letters – left side of chart:
Wide, narrow or irregular letters very close to each other.

Item 16

Letters close together with full 'o' and 'a'

mkd	mod	sli	sli	mod	mkd
LC	LB	LA	RA	RB	RC
●					

Letters close packed but irregularly formed with inhibited movement

mkd	mod	sli	sli	mod	mkd
LC	LB	LA	RA	RB	RC
X	●	X			

Firm, rapid movement but forms complicated and letters close together. Inflated and sealed 'o' and 'a'

mkd	mod	sli	sli	mod	mkd
LC	LB	LA	RA	RB	RC
●					

Wide-apart letters – right side of chart:
Letters wide apart and connected or with aerial connections.

Letters quite far apart in connected, simplified handwriting, the distance between letters increasing at the end of the word in the 'ing'. A sign of speed.

mkd	mod	sli	sli	mod	mkd
LC	LB	LA	RA	RB	RC
				●	

Letters far apart and disconnected but with some aerial continuity

mkd	mod	sli	sli	mod	mkd
LC	LB	LA	RA	RB	RC
			X	●	X

Letters far apart but firmly connected by baseline. A sign of flexibility rather than great speed

mkd	mod	sli	sli	mod	mkd
LC	LB	LA	RA	RB	RC
			X	●	X

CATEGORY THREE
20–28 REGULARITY

This category analyses regularity and irregularity.

Irregularity can be caused by tense or uncertain movements of the pen but also by lack of restraint, and should be marked on the left side of the chart. Regular forms in good order tend to be produced by a writing movement that is either naturally placid or extremely controlled, and should be marked on the right side of the chart.

The nine items within Category Three are:

20 Alignment
21 Regularity of word spacing
22 Regularity of margins
23 Regularity of 'i'-dots
24 Regularity of slant

25 Regularity of Middle Zone height
26 Regularity of Lower Zone
27 Pressure disturbance
28 Curve disturbance

		mkd	mod	sli	sli	mod	mkd		
		LC	LB	LA	RA	RB	RC		
Lines or words unparallel	20							20	Lines or words parallel
Irregular word spacing	21							21	Regular word spacing
Irregular margins	22							22	Regular margins
Irregular 'i'-dots	23							23	Regular 'i'-dots
Irregular slant	24							24	Regular slant
Irregular MZ height	25							25	Regular MZ height
Irregular LZ	26							26	Regular LZ
Disturbed pressure	27							27	Undisturbed pressure
Disturbed curves	28							28	Undisturbed curves

Item 20 Alignment
Lines or words unparallel or Lines and words parallel

Lines that are not parallel or contain words that hop about are signs of disorderly layout, and are marked on the left side of the chart.

Parallel lines are a sign of orderly layout. They can be horizontal, ascending, descending or undulating but provided they are parallel they are marked on the right side of the chart.

Watch out for signs that the writer has used a *guideline*! If the distance between the straight lines is perfectly equal and the writing obviously slow (0-16L) this is very likely and the mark should be on the middle line.

Handwriting on *ruled paper* should also be marked on the middle line, unless words, syllables and even lines rise above or descend below the ruled lines, in which case the left side of the chart should be marked.

What to look for

Lines or words unparallel – left side of chart:

Lines not parallel, words hopping within lines (example reduced).

Unparallel lines; slope increasing with each line

Words hopping within unparallel undulating lines ('criticism', 'little', 'about')

Lines not parallel

Item 20 ▲

mkd	mod	sli	sli	mod	mkd
LC	LB	LA	RA	RB	RC
	●				

mkd	mod	sli	sli	mod	mkd
LC	LB	LA	RA	RB	RC
	●				

Ruled lines not kept to in fast writing

mkd	mod	sli	sli	mod	mkd
LC	LB	LA	RA	RB	RC
●					

Lines or words parallel – right side of chart:

Lines and words within them parallel, and either straight or rising.

Lines parallel and horizontal. Words following direction of line. Baseline even

mkd	mod	sli	sli	mod	mkd
LC	LB	LA	RA	RB	RC
					●

33

Lines parallel and rising. Words following direction of line

réponds à Londres, afin de vous remercier cation opportune que vous avez apportée

mkd	mod	sli	sli	mod	mkd
LC	LB	LA	RA	RB	RC
					●

Item 21 Regularity of Word Spacing
Irregular word spacing or Regular word spacing

Irregular word spacing can vary from slight unevenness to words bunched together alternating with great gaps. When the word spacing is as irregular as this 'rivers' can be formed, that is, a gap in the same place in several succeeding lines makes the shape of a river in the surrounding dry land of words (example below). All irregular word spacing should be marked on the left side of the chart.

Regular word spacing is easy if the words are close together in a controlled writing. When they are regular in a widely spaced streamlined writing this shows an underlying order in the movement. Both these are signs of regularity and should be marked on the right side of the chart.

What to look for
Irregular word spacing – left side of chart:
Words irregularly spaced; sometimes forming 'rivers'.

Irregular word spacing forming a 'river' in the page layout

Item 21

mkd	mod	sli	sli	mod	mkd
LC	LB	LA	RA	RB	RC
	●				

Word spacing irregular

*here are different conceptions
nds a love song ought to have.
l impression is a hopeless w*

mkd	mod	sli	sli	mod	mkd
LC	LB	LA	RA	RB	RC
●					

Regular word spacing – right side of chart:
Regular spaces between words in close-packed or widely spaced writing.

Regular word spacing has not been difficult to achieve here because words are close together

*your letter pa
great pleasure. I
relieved & delighted
you are really poin
do English, I also
pleased by the tone
letter. you say that*

mkd	mod	sli	sli	mod	mkd
LC	LB	LA	RA	RB	RC
				●	

Fairly regular word spacing; more difficult to achieve because of wider spaces in a streamlined writing and therefore more significant

but one thing at a t

mkd	mod	sli	sli	mod	mkd
LC	LB	LA	RA	RB	RC
				●	

Item 22 Regularity of margins
Irregular margins or Regular margins

This item deals particularly with the left margin; the right margin is nearly always slightly irregular but when its irregularity is extreme this should be taken into account. The left margin can be jagged from line to line which is often associated with an agitated movement, or it can be undulating which usually goes with inhibited uncertain movement but can sometimes occur when the movement is otherwise well-controlled. All these signs of irregularity should be marked on the left side of the chart.

A regular left margin is often vertical but can also be oblique, that is, increasing steadily. In some cases the writer tries to produce not just a neat left margin but a neat right margin as well. all these signs of regularity should be marked on the right side of the chart.

What to look for

Irregular margins – left side of chart:

Left margin undulating, jagged or uncertain: sometimes right margin also irregular.

Right margin irregular: 'happy', 'your' and 'lovely' could have been at the end of the line. Left margin not really irregular so crosses

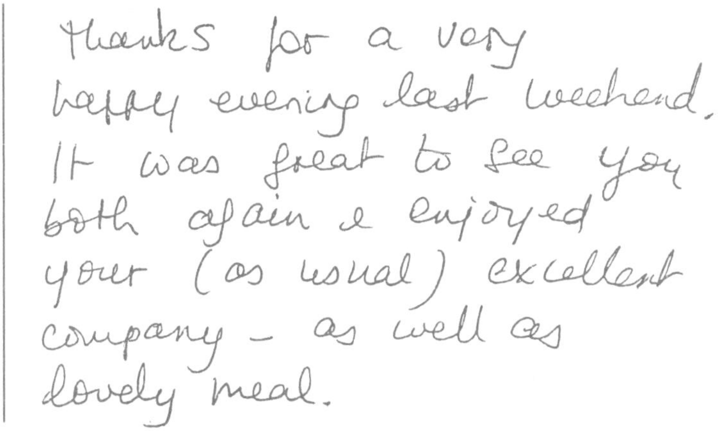

Irregular left margin undulating, uncertain, associated with uncertain movement

mkd	mod	sli	sli	mod	mkd
LC	LB	LA	RA	RB	RC
●					

mkd	mod	sli	sli	mod	mkd
LC	LB	LA	RA	RB	RC
	x	●	x		

[handwritten sample:]
Thanks for a very happy evening last weekend. It was great to see you both again & enjoyed your (as usual) excellent company – as well as lovely meal.

Regular margins – right side of chart:

Left margin regular, either vertical or oblique; sometimes right margin regular too.

Regular left margin

Regular oblique left margin as a result of quick writing movement

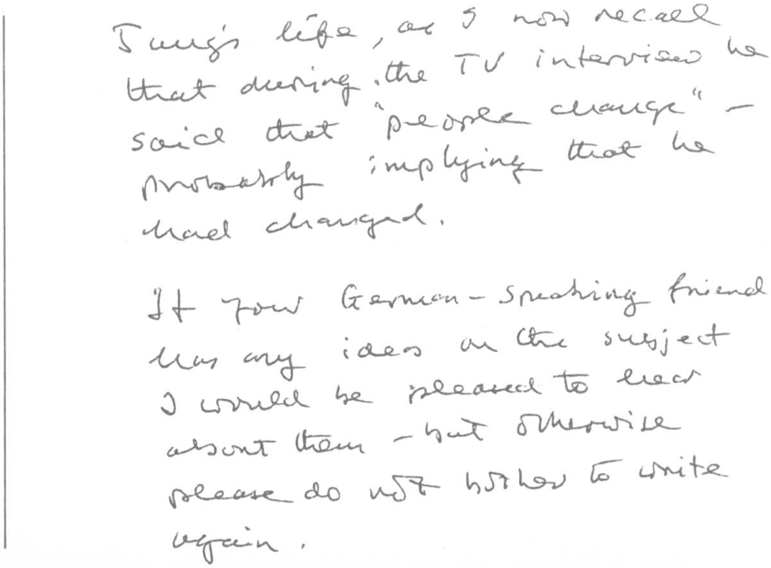

mkd	mod	sli	sli	mod	mkd
LC	LB	LA	RA	RB	RC
					●

mkd	mod	sli	sli	mod	mkd
LC	LB	LA	RA	RB	RC
			●		

[handwritten sample:]
Jung's life, as I now recall that during the TV interview he said that "people change" – probably implying that he had changed.

If your German-speaking friend has any ideas on the subject I would be pleased to hear about them – but otherwise please do not bother to write again.

Regular right margin as well as left margin because of the writer's aesthetical concern

20ᵗʰ Aug, '84.

Dear Mr. Desenclos,

Please forgive this intrusion into your busy schedule, but my sister gave me a copy of the outline to your course, and I was, to say the least, fascinated; particularly in view of the possibility of applying such a form of analysis to my pupils' work (not for any specific purpose – merely as a chance to see the possible value of such an exercise).

As it would not be possible for me to attend any of your lectures/workshops, I wonder if you could offer me any advice on how to study this

mkd	mod	sli	sli	mod	mkd
LC	LB	LA	RA	RB	RC
					●

Item 23 Regularity of 'i'-dots
Irregular 'i'-dots or Regular 'i'-dots

The 'i'-dot is a very tiny part of handwriting and is hardly ever consciously placed, so it can reveal much about the general movement of the writing.

When 'i'-dots are placed before or after or a long way from the stem they are irregular. This is common in irregular writing but can occur in regular writing. They can sometimes take an irregular form such as a dash or a wing-shape. All these irregularities should be marked on the left side of the chart.

The regular placing and form of 'i'-dots is frequent in irregular handwriting but can sometimes occur unexpectedly in regular handwriting. In both cases this characteristic should be marked on the right side of the chart.

What to look for
Irregular 'i'-dots – left side of chart:
'i'-dots irregular in position and/or form in irregular or regular handwriting.

Irregular position of 'i'-dots in regular handwriting

with similar interests.

Item 23

mkd	mod	sli	sli	mod	mkd
LC	LB	LA	RA	RB	RC
	●				

'i'-dots varying in form and position in irregular handwriting

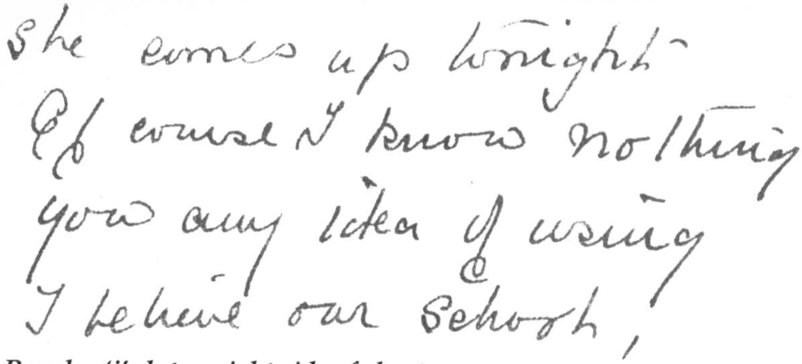

[handwritten sample]

mkd	mod	sli	sli	mod	mkd
LC	LB	LA	RA	RB	RC
	●				

Regular 'i'-dots – right side of chart:
'i'-dots regular in position and form in regular or irregular handwriting.

'i'-dots directly above the stem and not too high in fairly regular writing

[handwritten sample]

mkd	mod	sli	sli	mod	mkd
LC	LB	LA	RA	RB	RC
				●	

'i'-dots placed directly above the stem or nearly so in otherwise very irregular handwriting

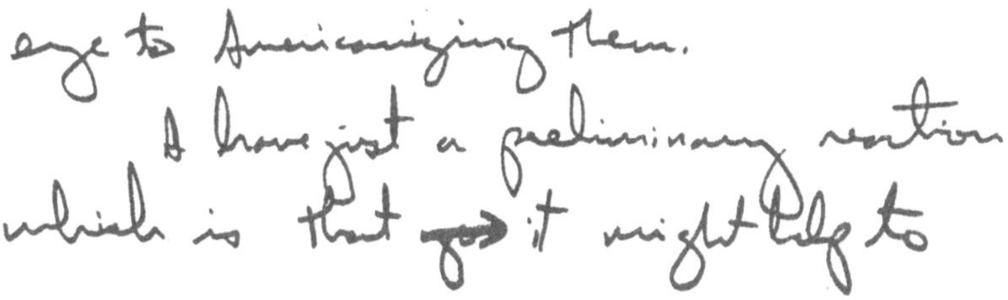

[handwritten sample]

mkd	mod	sli	sli	mod	mkd
LC	LB	LA	RA	RB	RC
				●	

Item 24 Regularity of Slant
Irregular slant or Regular slant

Whereas Item 14 (see page 29) covered the flexibility versus the stiffness and also the direction of the slant, the question here is the parallelism versus the discordance of the downstroke movement.

Discordance of slant, that is, downstrokes slanted now to the right, now to the left, should be marked on the left side of the chart. Moderate fluctuations should also be marked on the left not far from the middle line.

When the downstrokes are parallel, or nearly so, this should be marked on the right side of the chart, whether the writing is upright, slanted rightward or slanted leftward.

What to look for
Irregular slant – left side of chart:

Downstrokes slanting now right now left in clashing or fluctuating movement.

Clashing slant in all zones, especially upper and lower. Jerky, disturbed movement

Item 24

mkd	mod	sli	sli	mod	mkd
LC	LB	LA	RA	RB	RC
●					

MZ downstrokes irregular because of flowing movement. Flexible irregularity

mkd	mod	sli	sli	mod	mkd
LC	LB	LA	RA	RB	RC
		●			

Regular slant – right side of chart:

Downstrokes parallel with right or left slant or upright.

Slant of downstrokes parallel in all zones. Measured, regular movement

mkd	mod	sli	sli	mod	mkd
LC	LB	LA	RA	RB	RC
				●	

Downstrokes parallel in long strokes of UZ and LZ but not in MZ because of rapid movement

mkd	mod	sli	sli	mod	mkd
LC	LB	LA	RA	RB	RC
		X	●		X

Parallel downstrokes with a leftward slant

mkd	mod	sli	sli	mod	mkd
LC	LB	LA	RA	RB	RC
			●		

Parallel downstrokes in upright handwriting

mkd	mod	sli	sli	mod	mkd
LC	LB	LA	RA	RB	RC
			●		

Item 25 Regularity of Middle Zone Height
Irregular Middle Zone height or Regular Middle Zone height

The height of Middle Zone letters can be anything from almost completely uneven to extremely even. Letters formed with a simple up and down movement (such as 'm' or 'n') are particularly important for judging it but other letters should also be considered.

Some handwritings show irregular Middle Zone letters on a horizontal baseline, whereas in others letters are hopping out of the line. In both cases the mark should be on the left side.

In contrast there are handwritings in which every letter inside the word and every word inside the line show a measured regularity as if between double lines. Both evenness of this degree and a reasonable regularity of Middle Zone height should be marked on the right side of the chart.

What to look for
Irregular MZ height – left side of chart:

MZ height slightly to extremely uneven. On horizontal baseline or hopping out of line.

Uneven MZ height 'o' and 'a' small, 'n' and 'm' slightly larger. Baseline uneven but with fluent movement

Item 25

mkd	mod	sli	sli	mod	mkd
LC	LB	LA	RA	RB	RC
	●				

Uneven MZ height ('a', 'o' and MZ of 'd' large, 'n' and 'u' small). Baseline uneven and movement animated

mkd	mod	sli	sli	mod	mkd
LC	LB	LA	RA	RB	RC
●					

Inequality in a very small MZ. Tense, jerky movement with horizontal baseline

mkd	mod	sli	sli	mod	mkd
LC	LB	LA	RA	RB	RC
●					

Very uneven, written in haste. Hopping letters, but rhythmical and effervescent writing movement

mkd	mod	sli	sli	mod	mkd
LC	LB	LA	RA	RB	RC
●					

Regular MZ height – right side of chart:

MZ height even, sometimes as if between double lines.

MZ letters even on even baseline and feeling of being between double lines

mkd	mod	sli	sli	mod	mkd
LC	LB	LA	RA	RB	RC
				●	

Regular MZ with a firm stroke movement

mkd	mod	sli	sli	mod	mkd
LC	LB	LA	RA	RB	RC
				●	

Item 26 Regularity of Lower Zone
Irregular Lower Zone or Regular Lower Zone

The Lower Zone can be irregular in many different ways, in size, form, slant or pressure. In some handwritings there is one persistent disturbance, such as spasm, unusual length etc. In others several different irregularities can be seen. Both kinds of Lower Zone irregularity are marked on the left side of the chart.

Absolute regularity in the Lower Zone is rare, but if the writer consistently uses a certain form, whether a slender or full loop or a graceful unlooped curve or a straight unlooped Lower Zone, these regular and marked on the right side of the chart.

What to look for
Irregular LZ – left side of chart:

One persistent irregularity or several different ones. Can be irregular in size, form, slant or pressure.

Item 26

Persistent irregularity in slant

mkd	mod	sli	sli	mod	mkd
LC	LB	LA	RA	RB	RC
	●				

Irregularities in form, slant and fullness

mkd	mod	sli	sli	mod	mkd
LC	LB	LA	RA	RB	RC
●					

Irregularity of form evident in 'of' in first, second and fourth lines. Pressure irregular. Clubbed endings: 'nothing' in first line, 'any' in the second. Lengths irregular: compare 'may' and 'staff' in fourth line. Jerk in 'High' in third line. This handwriting sample has been reduced

mkd	mod	sli	sli	mod	mkd
LC	LB	LA	RA	RB	RC
●					

Regular LZ – right side of chart:

Regular slender or full loops, or regular without loops.

LZ loops regular in form, length, fullness, slant and pressure, and connected to following MZ letter

mkd	mod	sli	sli	mod	mkd
LC	LB	LA	RA	RB	RC
				●	

LZ loops gracefully curved and unconnected

mkd	mod	sli	sli	mod	mkd
LC	LB	LA	RA	RB	RC
				●	

LZ loops fuller than copybook style, but consistent and appropriate to the writing

mkd	mod	sli	sli	mod	mkd
LC	LB	LA	RA	RB	RC
				●	

Unlooped and regular LZ

mkd	mod	sli	sli	mod	mkd
LC	LB	LA	RA	RB	RC
				●	

Item 27 Pressure Disturbance
Disturbed pressure or Undisturbed pressure

Pressure is undisturbed when it comes in the expected place, that is, on the downstroke, because the writing movement that produces pressure on the downstroke must be reasonably regular.

When pressure appears on the upstroke or on a lateral stroke this is a sign that the pressure is disturbed and the writing movement irregular. This applies even more when there is pressure on only part of a stroke, or when the end of a stroke looks like a club. Disturbed pressure can also appear in the Upper Zone, especially in 't'-bars, or in the projections of the Lower Zone. All these should be marked on the left of the chart.

Handwriting with undisturbed pressure can either show a rhythmical alternation between pressure on downstroke and release on upstroke (modulated), or it can show as much pressure on the upstroke as on the downstroke with a restrained writing movement (unmodulated). This is described in Item 12 but for the purposes of Item 27 both modulated and unmodulated pressure are considered as undisturbed provided there is not more pressure on the upstroke than on the downstroke. Both should be marked on the right side of the chart.

What to look for
Disturbed pressure – left side of chart:
Pressure not on downstroke but on upstroke ('reversed'), or on lateral stroke or 't'-bars. Spasm or clubbing.

Spasm in the curl of '5th' and in the LZ where the endings are also clubbed

Item 27

mkd	mod	sli	sli	mod	mkd
LC	LB	LA	RA	RB	RC
	●				

Reversed pressure: often more pressure on upstrokes than downstrokes

mkd	mod	sli	sli	mod	mkd
LC	LB	LA	RA	RB	RC
●					

Pressure on downstroke ('modulated') and sometimes on upstroke as well ('unmodulated').

Pressure undisturbed and light. Slightly less pressure on upstroke than on downstroke

will have to be

mkd	mod	sli	sli	mod	mkd
LC	LB	LA	RA	RB	RC
					●

Rhythmical pressure with a flexible nib

mine will be

mkd	mod	sli	sli	mod	mkd
LC	LB	LA	RA	RB	RC
				●	

Rhythmical, modulated pressure

can do to help,

mkd	mod	sli	sli	mod	mkd
LC	LB	LA	RA	RB	RC
					●

Item 28 Curve Disturbance
Disturbed curves or Undisturbed curves

Some writers find it difficult to form curves and produce angles instead; others distort not just the curves but strokes that are meant to be straight, and some writings show tremors, jerks and other agitated movements. All these are signs of irregularity and should be marked on the left side of the chart.

If a handwriting shows impeccable curves with practically no disturbance in their form the writing movement must have been either calm or superlatively controlled and very regular, so the mark on the chart should be well to the right. If the curves are still shapely but softer and less regular the mark should still be on the right but nearer the middle line.

What to look for
Disturbed curves – left side of chart:

Curves distorted, unintended angles, twisted strokes, jerks or tremors.

Distorted curves, jerks as in the 'p' of 'help'

I think this would help with problems eye. Basically, the language

Item 28

mkd	mod	sli	sli	mod	mkd
LC	LB	LA	RA	RB	RC
●					

Twisted deformed downstrokes and upstrokes, especially in long letters;
eg 'cheval', 'les', 'decontractes'; unintended angles

mkd	mod	sli	sli	mod	mkd
LC	LB	LA	RA	RB	RC
●					

Tremors, due to old age in this case

mkd	mod	sli	sli	mod	mkd
LC	LB	LA	RA	RB	RC
●					

Undisturbed curves – right side of chart:
Curves smooth and impeccably controlled or still shapely but
softer and less regular.

Impeccably rounded
forms without tension

mkd	mod	sli	sli	mod	mkd
LC	LB	LA	RA	RB	RC
					●

Rounded with energetic up and down movement

mkd	mod	sli	sli	mod	mkd
LC	LB	LA	RA	RB	RC
					●

Rounded forms, slightly deformed by haste

mkd	mod	sli	sli	mod	mkd
LC	LB	LA	RA	RB	RC
		X	●	X	

Well-rounded loops in UZ and LZ; but not in MZ

now you'll be able
I just hope you don't have

mkd	mod	sli	sli	mod	mkd
LC	LB	LA	RA	RB	RC
		✗	●	✗	

CATEGORY FOUR
30–36 EXPANSIVENESS OF MOVEMENT

Expansiveness is characterized by lively sweeping stroke movements that fill the available space; restrained movement by limited stroke movements that leave spaces empty.

A restrained stroke movement produces short, narrow letter forms and lines that often stop before the edge of the page. The Lower Zone and Upper Zone projections are short and do not overlap or touch. These characteristics may result from firm mental control in fast writing or from a tight, subdued movement in slow writing and are marked on the left side of the chart.

An expansive stroke movement produces lively sweeping strokes, up-and-down or lateral or both. One or two the zones can be oversized or inflated, which can lead to overlapping lines, and the page can be filled to the very edge on the right. These characteristics should be marked on the right side of the chart.

The seven items in Category Four are:

30 Fullness of the Middle Zone ovals
31 Width of right margin
32 Animation of movement
33 Length of the Lower Zone
34 Fullness of the Lower Zone
35 Space between interline projections
36 Height of 'i'-dots.

		mkd	mod	sli	sli	mod	mkd		
		LC	LB	LA	RA	RB	RC		
Lean MZ ovals	30							30	Full MZ ovals
Wide right margin	31							31	No right margin
Limited movement (any zone)	32							32	Animated movement (any zone)
Short LZ	33							33	Long LZ
Lean LZ	34							34	Full LZ
Clear interlines	35							35	Overlapping projections
Low 'i'-dots	36							36	High 'i'-dots

Item 30 Fullness of Middle Zone Ovals
Lean Middle Zone ovals or Full Middle Zone ovals

This item considers oval letters and parts of letters in the Middle Zone, such as 'o', 'a', 'q', 'g' and 'd'.

When the Middle Zone ovals are lean this can happen consistently right through the handwriting or can be occasional and mixed with fuller Middle Zone ovals. It can be associated with fullness or leanness in the Upper Zone and Lower Zone. Sometimes the Middle Zone oval is so lean that it can be mistaken for an undotted 'i'. These should be marked on the left side of the chart.

Full Middle Zone ovals are well-rounded and surround a clear area, that is, they are not blurred or ink-filled. Exaggerated Middle Zone ovals are inflated into circles or stretched horizontally. The top of the oval can be open or closed. All these should be marked on the right side of the chart.

What to look for
Lean MZ ovals – left side of chart:

Lean MZ ovals with lean or full UZ or LZ.
Lean MZ ovals mixed with full (see eg in 30R).

Item 30

Lean MZ ovals in lean handwriting

mkd	mod	sli	sli	mod	mkd
LC	LB	LA	RA	RB	RC
●					

In this word 'Gatwick' the 'a' is as lean as the 'i'

mkd	mod	sli	sli	mod	mkd
LC	LB	LA	RA	RB	RC
●					

Lean MZ ovals with full UZ and LZ loops

mkd	mod	sli	sli	mod	mkd
LC	LB	LA	RA	RB	RC
●					

Full MZ ovals – right side of chart:

MZ ovals full, sometimes circular or stretched. Top of oval open or closed. Mixed lean and full MZ ovals.

Inflated MZ ovals with circular 'o's in 'you' and 'our', while 'n' and 'u' are very narrow

mkd	mod	sli	sli	mod	mkd
LC	LB	LA	RA	RB	RC
					●

MZ ovals horizontally stretched

mkd	mod	sli	sli	mod	mkd
LC	LB	LA	RA	RB	RC
					●

Full MZ ovals open on top

mkd	mod	sli	sli	mod	mkd
LC	LB	LA	RA	RB	RC
					●

Relatively full MZ ovals in otherwise narrow writing

mkd	mod	sli	sli	mod	mkd
LC	LB	LA	RA	RB	RC
		X	●	X	

Mixed lean ('having') and full ('enjoyed' and 'your') MZ ovals

mkd	mod	sli	sli	mod	mkd
LC	LB	LA	RA	RB	RC
		X	●	X	

Item 31 Width of right Margin
Wide right margin or No right margin

Some writers stop every line unnecessarily before the right edge, leaving a wide right margin (regular or not). This should be marked on the left side of the chart.

But when a handwriting spreads to the very edge of the page on every line, leaving no right margin, this should be marked on the right side of the chart. This is still more so when the whole page is invaded from left to right.

What to look for
Wide right margin – left side of chart:
Lines stop unnecessarily before right edge of page.

Wide, uneven right margin, some long strokes at ends of lines

mkd	mod	sli	sli	mod	mkd
LC	LB	LA	RA	RB	RC
●					

No right margin – right side of chart:
Lines invading whole page to right edge of page and even making almost no left margin; or lines spreading to right edge of page with normal left margin.

Left margin quite narrow but no right margin

No right margin but left margin normal in width

mkd	mod	sli	sli	mod	mkd
LC	LB	LA	RA	RB	RC
					●

mkd	mod	sli	sli	mod	mkd
LC	LB	LA	RA	RB	RC
			●		

Item 32 Animation of Movement
Limited movement (any zone) or Animated movement (any zone)

Whether the movement is animated or limited can be seen in the size and length of the strokes and the fullness or leanness of the curves.

In sober, inhibited handwriting the movement is limited so that the writing in general tends to be small and lean with short Upper Zone and Lower Zone and short ending strokes. These features should be marked on the left side of the chart.

Animated writing movement shows itself in sweeping strokes and sometimes also in inflated curves and loops. The Middle Zone is sometimes full but can have a vigorous, streamlined lateral flow. The Lower Zone is often full and long and even the Upper Zone, which is far from the body and therefore requires more effort, can be full of soaring strokes. Although the animated movement is fast by definition the number of words per minute may be relatively low because of time wasted on exaggerations. Both streamlined and inflated examples should be marked on the right side of the chart.

What to look for
Limited movement (any zone) – left side of chart:
Small, lean writing, sometimes short UZ and LZ and short ending strokes.

Very small writing with very small MZ and UZ but longer though lean LZ

Item 32

mkd	mod	sli	sli	mod	mkd
LC	LB	LA	RA	RB	RC
●					

Small writing with UZ and LZ shorter than MZ. Word endings short

[handwritten sample]

mkd	mod	sli	sli	mod	mkd
LC	LB	LA	RA	RB	RC
●					

Normal size handwriting but with most endings cut short

[handwritten sample]

mkd	mod	sli	sli	mod	mkd
LC	LB	LA	RA	RB	RC
	●				

Animated movement (any zone) – right side of chart:
Sweeping strokes showing in up and down movement, in inflated loops in any zone, or in lateral movement.

Lateral animation, inflated lassos, and hyperconnections

[handwritten sample]

mkd	mod	sli	sli	mod	mkd
LC	LB	LA	RA	RB	RC
					●

This handwriting of a woman in her eighties shows animated movement: flying stroke in the 't'-bar of 'thoroughly'; inflated loop in the 'j' of 'enjoyed'; soaring initial stroke in the 'n' of 'novelty'; lasso in the 't' of 'to'; lateral hyperconnection between 'it' and 'was' and between 'to' and 'your'. But as there is some leanness in the MZ – eg the 'o' of 'thoroughly' – this counteracts the exaggerations and the chart is marked with crosses on RCD (for the exaggerations) and middle line (for the comparative leanness), the mark itself being on RB. Such counteracting leanness is a characteristic of effervescence, rather like a short dance step between leaps

[handwritten sample]

mkd	mod	sli	sli	mod	mkd
LC	LB	LA	RA	RB	RC
		✗		●	✗

Item 33 Length of the Lower Zone
Short Lower Zone or Long Lower Zone

This zone is the easiest to form as it involves downward movements towards the body. Even so, some writers keep the Lower Zone shorter than the Upper Zone. A short Lower Zone is a sign of limited movement and so should be marked on the left side of the chart. A long or excessively long Lower Zone is a sign of expansive movement and should be marked on the right side of the chart.

What to look for
Short LZ – left side of chart:

LZ shorter than MZ because of limited movement and sometimes speed as well. Sometimes shorter than UZ.

LZ and UZ very short, MZ large

, right margin to

mkd	mod	sli	sli	mod	mkd
LC	LB	LA	RA	RB	RC
●					

LZ and UZ both very short, MZ somewhat larger but obscured by use of felt-tip pen

being possibly

mkd	mod	sli	sli	mod	mkd
LC	LB	LA	RA	RB	RC
●					

Faster but still accurate handwriting with short LZ, UZ which is longer but not excessively so

importants a faire

mkd	mod	sli	sli	mod	mkd
LC	LB	LA	RA	RB	RC
●					

Long LZ – right side of chart:

LZ longer than UZ or MZ or longer than both together.

LZ exaggeratedly long, longer than MZ and UZ together

buddy. g'ind

mkd	mod	sli	sli	mod	mkd
LC	LB	LA	RA	RB	RC
					●

LZ and UZ both long

with lots of

mkd	mod	sli	sli	mod	mkd
LC	LB	LA	RA	RB	RC
				●	

Item 34 Fullness of the Lower Zone
Lean Lower Zone or Full Lower Zone

When the loops of the Lower Zone are very thin or are replaced by a single stroke this is usually because of a limited movement which does not find curves easy or because of stylization. A fast writing movement which does not waste time on inessentials can also produce a lean Lower Zone. All these should be marked on the left side of the chart.

Some writers choose the Lower Zone for full or even inflated loops which can be gracefully curved or unshapely, even nearly triangular. These should be marked on the right side of the chart.

Another fairly common form in the Lower Zone is a leftward-tending curve which is not connected to the next letter, usually graceful. When this curves up towards the Middle Zone it should be marked on the right side of the chart, when it is shorter and less curved asterisks should be used.

What to look for
Lean LZ – left side of chart:

Lean or no LZ loops because of limited movement, stylization or speed.

Slender loops, a little narrower than copybook

mkd	mod	sli	sli	mod	mkd
LC	LB	LA	RA	RB	RC
		●			

No loop, inhibited and stylized

mkd	mod	sli	sli	mod	mkd
LC	LB	LA	RA	RB	RC

Lean LZ but full MZ

mkd	mod	sli	sli	mod	mkd
LC	LB	LA	RA	RB	RC
	●				

Lean because of speed

mkd	mod	sli	sli	mod	mkd
LC	LB	LA	RA	RB	RC
●					

Full LZ – right side of chart:
LZ loops full, inflated or even nearly triangular; or gracefully curved up towards MZ but not connected.

LZ fuller than copybook model but not excessively so

mkd	mod	sli	sli	mod	mkd
LC	LB	LA	RA	RB	RC
			●		

LZ loops inflated and veering in shape between circular and triangular

mkd	mod	sli	sli	mod	mkd
LC	LB	LA	RA	RB	RC
					●

LZ gracefully curved up towards MZ but not connected

mkd	mod	sli	sli	mod	mkd
LC	LB	LA	RA	RB	RC
				●	

Item 35 Space Between Interline Projections
Clear interlines or Overlapping projections

If the Upper and Lower Zones do not project much into the space between the lines, this is a sign that the movement is limited either by restraint or simplification, and should be marked on the left side of the chart. The mark should be far to the left (LC) when the space between the handwritings is so clear that a ruled line can be drawn between them without touching any projection.

However, when the Upper Zone and Lower Zone stick out so far from their own lines that they overlap with those of the lines above and below, this is a sign of expansive movement and should be marked on the right side of the chart.

What to look for
Clear interlines – left side of chart:
Space between lines is clear because UZ and LZ projections are short in limited or streamlined writing.

Item 35

Clear interlines because writing is very small although LZ is comparatively long

mkd	mod	sli	sli	mod	mkd
LC	LB	LA	RA	RB	RC
●					

Large, streamlined handwriting with fairly long projections and adequate interline

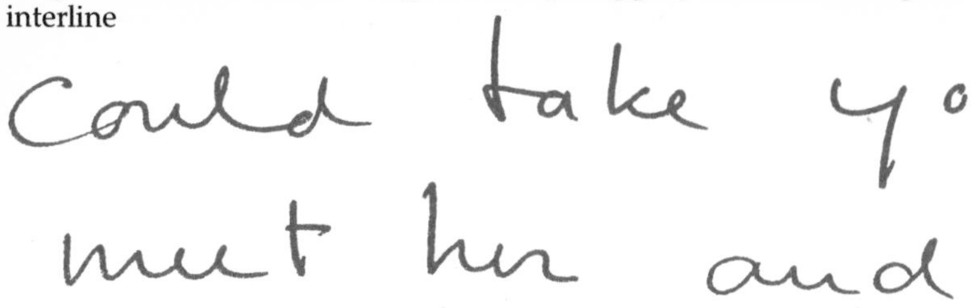

[handwriting: "Could take yo meet her and"]

mkd	mod	sli	sli	mod	mkd
LC	LB	LA	RA	RB	RC
	●				

Overlapping projections – right side of chart:

UZ and LZ projections in adjacent lines overlapping.

LZ so long that it stretches below the next line. UZ not exaggerated

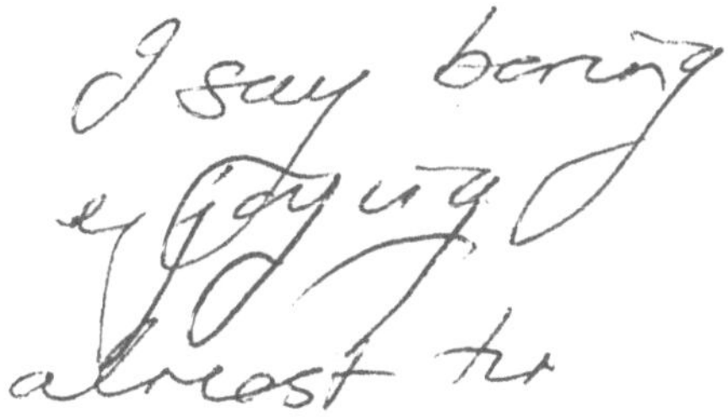

[handwriting: "I say boring ... almost the"]

mkd	mod	sli	sli	mod	mkd
LC	LB	LA	RA	RB	RC
					●

UZ sometimes touches line above. LZ not quite as long

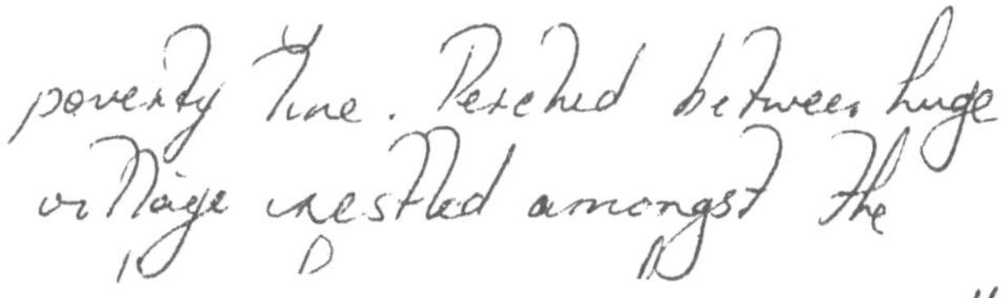

[handwriting: "poverty line. Perched between huge village nestled amongst the"]

mkd	mod	sli	sli	mod	mkd
LC	LB	LA	RA	RB	RC
				●	

Both extensions (UZ and LZ) are long and sometimes tangle. Unevenness of lines has increased the chances of this happening

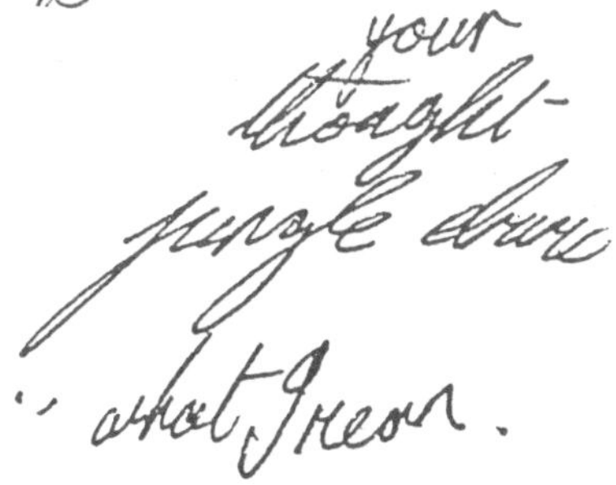

[handwriting: "your thought-jungle drum ... what I mean."]

mkd	mod	sli	sli	mod	mkd
LC	LB	LA	RA	RB	RC
					●

UZ and LZ long but only occasionally tangling

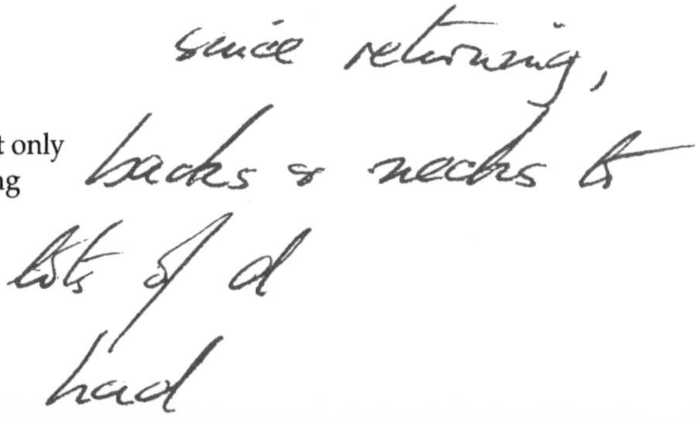

[handwriting: "since returning, backs & necks & lots of d had"]

mkd	mod	sli	sli	mod	mkd
LC	LB	LA	RA	RB	RC
				●	

Item 36 Height of 'i'-dots
Low 'i'-dots or High 'i'-dots

Economy in the writing movement leads to low 'i'-dots; these are either precisely placed just above their stems, or, in streamlined, simplified handwriting, can form a 'clever connection', placed low to join the next Middle Zone letter to increase speed. Both these should be marked on the left of the chart.

High positioning of 'i'-dots is often associated with animated movement in the Upper Zone. Paradoxically it can also occur in sober handwriting with a short Upper Zone, because Upper Zone projections proceed from a more conscious gesture than the one placing the 'i'-dots which are therefore freer from convention. High 'i'-dots should be marked on the right side of the chart.

What to look for
Low 'i'-dots – left side of chart:

'i'-dots low in restrained writing or low and joined to next letter by 'clever connection' in streamlined writing

Item 36

Neat handwriting with low 'i'-dots

just longing

mkd	mod	sli	sli	mod	mkd
LC	LB	LA	RA	RB	RC
●					

Streamlined handwriting with low 'i'-dots as simplified way of connecting with next letter

magination

mkd	mod	sli	sli	mod	mkd
LC	LB	LA	RA	RB	RC
	●				

Irregular writing with low, well-controlled 'i'-dots

still

is writing

mkd	mod	sli	sli	mod	mkd
LC	LB	LA	RA	RB	RC
●					

High 'i'-dots – right side of chart:

'i'-dots high in animated writing when they can be in form of a dash. Sometimes high in sober writing.

High 'i'-dots in animated writing, dashed rather than light

at a thought – that if

such a jot I take it

mkd	mod	sli	sli	mod	mkd
LC	LB	LA	RA	RB	RC
					●

High 'i'-dots in animated
writing, also sometimes
dashed but light

mkd	mod	sli	sli	mod	mkd
LC	LB	LA	RA	RB	RC
					●

'i'-dots very high, even higher
than the rest of the UZ in
otherwise controlled calligraphic
writing

mkd	mod	sli	sli	mod	mkd
LC	LB	LA	RA	RB	RC
					●

CATEGORY FIVE
40–46 FIRMNESS

This category deals with the firmness versus the looseness of the
writing movement (that is, a soft or weak movement).

The signs of loose writing movement are weak pressure with
roundness where straightness is conventionally required. Lines are
not straight. Thread, unfinished endings and omitted 't'-bars are
not exceptional. Words are sometimes far apart. All these should
be marked on the left side of the chart.

The signs of firm movement are resoluteness, pressure and
sharpness of the stroke. The straight downstroke generally results
in angular connective forms. Emphasis on 't'-bars and ending
strokes is common.

When the handwriting is fast as well as firm (sentence impulse),
energy and firmness are spent on the lines more than on particular
strokes. This makes the lines rigidly straight and the words close
together.

Both cases should be marked on the right of the chart.

The seven items in Category Five are:

40 Width of word spacing
41 Straightness of lines
42 Straightness of downstrokes
43 Pressure firmness
44 Stress on ending strokes
45 Stress on 't'-bars
46 Angularity

		mkd	mod	sli	sli	mod	mkd		
		LC	LB	LA	RA	RB	RC		
Wide space between words	40							40	Narrow space between words
Lines not straight	41							41	Lines straight
Downstrokes not straight	42							42	Downstrokes straight
Weak pressure	43							43	Strong pressure
Soft or unfinished endings	44							44	Stress on ending strokes
Weak or omitted 't'-bars	45							45	Stressed 't'-bars/cross-strokes
Soft rounded forms	46							46	Angular forms

Item 40 Width of Word Spacing
Wide space between words or Narrow space between words

This item deals with the actual space between words, not with the regularity versus the irregularity of this spacing which has been seen in Item 21.

In copybook handwriting there should be a space the size of a non-capital 'm' between each word and about twice that width between sentences. This can be taken as a rough guide, wider spaces being marked on the left side of the chart, narrower ones on the right. It goes without saying that the width of the handwriting itself should be taken into account.

What to look for
Wide space between words – left side of chart:
Wide space between words in either wide or narrow handwriting.

Widely spaced words in wide handwriting

Item 40

mkd	mod	sli	sli	mod	mkd
LC	LB	LA	RA	RB	RC
	●				

Widely spaced words in narrow handwriting

mkd	mod	sli	sli	mod	mkd
LC	LB	LA	RA	RB	RC
●					

Narrow space between words – right side of chart:
Words close together in narrow or wide handwriting.

Words close together in a narrow handwriting

mkd	mod	sli	sli	mod	mkd
LC	LB	LA	RA	RB	RC
					●

Words close together in a fairly wide handwriting

she has been too much (handwritten)

mkd	mod	sli	sli	mod	mkd
LC	LB	LA	RA	RB	RC
					●

Item 41 Straightness of Lines
Lines not straight or Lines straight

Lines which are not straight show lack of firmness and should be marked on the left side of the chart.

Straight lines are a sign of firmness in the writing movement. They can be straight and horizontal or straight and rising. In both cases the mark should be on the right side of the chart.

NB For possible use of a guideline see Item 20 on page 32.

What to look for
Lines not straight – left side of chart:

Lines undulating, concave or convex.

Undulating or wavy lines starting with a concave section: 'the business of settling'

Item 41

the business of settling in is whelming. Stay tight, mt of (handwritten)

mkd	mod	sli	sli	mod	mkd
LC	LB	LA	RA	RB	RC
●					

Second line concave

ad in today's paper thought it might be of interest to you. (handwritten)

mkd	mod	sli	sli	mod	mkd
LC	LB	LA	RA	RB	RC
		●			

Both lines convex, especially the second one

oup aimé l'Ecosse et les gens là-bas r pour voir la côte ouest des Highlands (handwritten)

mkd	mod	sli	sli	mod	mkd
LC	LB	LA	RA	RB	RC
●					

Lines straight – right side of chart:
Lines straight and horizontal or straight and rising.

58

Straight, horizontal lines

(handwriting sample)

mkd	mod	sli	sli	mod	mkd
LC	LB	LA	RA	RB	RC
				●	

Straight, rising lines

(handwriting sample)

mkd	mod	sli	sli	mod	mkd
LC	LB	LA	RA	RB	RC
					●

Item 42 Straightness of Downstrokes
Downstrokes not straight or Downstrokes straight

When downstrokes which are expected to be straight are curved, wavy or twisty this shows a lack of firmness and should be marked on the left side of the chart.

When the downstroke is very straight, causing angular forms, this is a sign of firmness and should be marked on the right side of the chart. Sometimes, however, long downstrokes (of bizonal or trizonal letters) are firmer than those of the small Middle Zone letters. Then asterisks must be used.

What to look for
Downstrokes not straight – left side of chart:
Downstrokes curved, soft or twisting when they are meant to be straight.

Item 42

Flexible, curved downstroke movement in all zones. No straight segments

(handwriting sample)

mkd	mod	sli	sli	mod	mkd
LC	LB	LA	RA	RB	RC
●					

Soft, curved downstrokes

(handwriting sample)

mkd	mod	sli	sli	mod	mkd
LC	LB	LA	RA	RB	RC
●					

Unintentional curves or twists

(handwriting sample)

mkd	mod	sli	sli	mod	mkd
LC	LB	LA	RA	RB	RC
●					

Downstrokes straight – right side of chart:

Downstrokes straight in all zones or less straight in MZ.

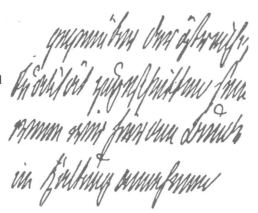

Straight downstrokes in all zones, especially MZ where they are also long. (The writing of Bismarck)

mkd	mod	sli	sli	mod	mkd
LC	LB	LA	RA	RB	RC
					●

The downstrokes are very straight in long letters, less so in MZ because of the speed

mkd	mod	sli	sli	mod	mkd
LC	LB	LA	RA	RB	RC
			X	●	X

The downstrokes are straight in long letters but the movement is fairly soft in MZ

mkd	mod	sli	sli	mod	mkd
LC	LB	LA	RA	RB	RC
		X		●	X

Item 43 Pressure Firmness
Weak pressure or Strong pressure

This item deals with the strength versus the weakness of pressure as a sign of firmness of the writing movement.

Weak pressure can be seen when the stroke, especially the Middle Zone downstroke, is pale or blurred. This can be caused by feebleness of movement or by slackness. Both should be marked on the left side of the chart. Slight pressure, that is, thin but fairly resolute strokes, should be marked near the middle line.

Strong pressure can be seen when the stroke is reasonably thick or, when a Biro has been used, there is a welt visible on the back of the paper which can be felt. Some wide nibs, especially in felt pens, can produce a thick stroke movement without much pressure but the firmness can usually be judged by the firm shape of the surrounding strokes. This strong pressure can occur mainly on the downstroke, with a lighter pressure on other strokes giving a rhythmical movement, or it can occur monotonously on all strokes or spasmodically in unexpected places. While each of these places gives a slightly different meaning to the strong pressure, what matters most in this item is the degree of firmness, and all these signs of strong pressure should be marked on the right side of the chart.

What to look for

Weak pressure – left side of chart:
Stroke pale or blurred with feeble or slack movement. Slight pressure with thin, fairly resolute stroke.

Lack of pressure with slack and feeble movement in blurred stroke

[handwriting sample]

Item 43

mkd	mod	sli	sli	mod	mkd
LC	LB	LA	RA	RB	RC
●					

Slight pressure, thin but fairly resolute strokes with some stiffness

[handwriting sample]

mkd	mod	sli	sli	mod	mkd
LC	LB	LA	RA	RB	RC
●					

Strong pressure – right side of chart:
Thickness of stroke from pressure on downstroke or upstroke or both or lateral or part of stroke.

Invariably heavy pressure

[handwriting sample]

mkd	mod	sli	sli	mod	mkd
LC	LB	LA	RA	RB	RC
				●	

Pressure strong on downstrokes, lighter on upstrokes and lateral strokes

[handwriting sample]

mkd	mod	sli	sli	mod	mkd
LC	LB	LA	RA	RB	RC
				●	

Strong unequal pressure in effervescent writing

Hope you haven't already got it !

mkd	mod	sli	sli	mod	mkd
LC	LB	LA	RA	RB	RC
					●

Pressure sometimes spasmodic on accessory strokes and in LZ

I'm sure is Tough!. I don't even remember hardly pressing, and the

mkd	mod	sli	sli	mod	mkd
LC	LB	LA	RA	RB	RC
				X	X

Item 44 Stress on Ending Strokes
Soft or unfinished endings or Stress on ending strokes

Ending strokes without stress can be soft and thready in a streamlined handwriting or short without pressure and unfinished in a restrained handwriting. Both kinds should be marked on the left side of the chart.

Stress on ending strokes shows itself in two possible kinds of pressure: either decreasing sharply, forming a point; or stopping abruptly with an increase in thickness which can vary according to the pen used. Straightness and length of the ending strokes are additional expressions of stress. All these should be marked on the right side of the chart.

What to look for
Soft or unfinished endings – left side of chart:
Ending stroke unfinished as part of a limited movement, or soft in a cursive writing.

Both words end with unfinished 'e' _telephone have_

Item 44

mkd	mod	sli	sli	mod	mkd
LC	LB	LA	RA	RB	RC
●					

Soft endings, almost thread-like, in cursive handwriting

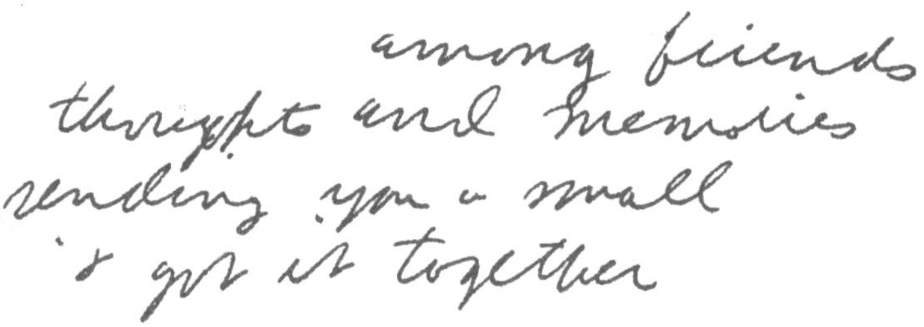

[handwriting samples]

mkd	mod	sli	sli	mod	mkd
LC	LB	LA	RA	RB	RC
		●			

Stress on ending strokes – right side of chart:

Ending strokes, sharply pointed, clawed, ending with abrupt thickness or long and straight.

Ending strokes sharply pointed

[handwriting: you can judge,]

mkd	mod	sli	sli	mod	mkd
LC	LB	LA	RA	RB	RC
				●	

Ending stroke of 'than' clawed

[handwriting: Rather than]

mkd	mod	sli	sli	mod	mkd
LC	LB	LA	RA	RB	RC
				●	

Ending strokes abrupt and thick

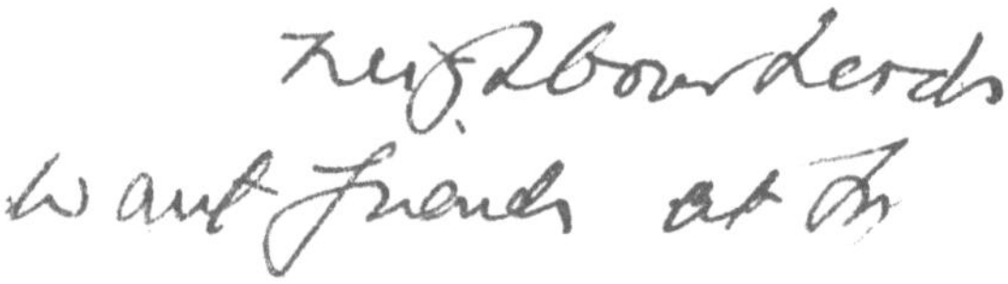

[handwriting: Neighbourhoods / we want friends at h]

mkd	mod	sli	sli	mod	mkd
LC	LB	LA	RA	RB	RC
			X	●	X

Two ending strokes extended (one straight, the other sharply pointed), one cut very short

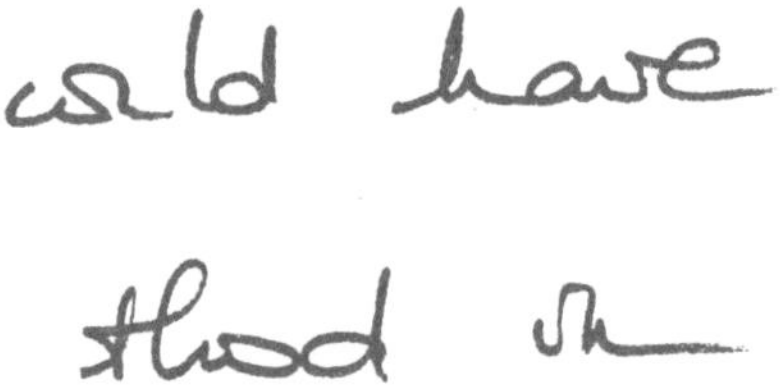

[handwriting: would have / flood on]

mkd	mod	sli	sli	mod	mkd
LC	LB	LA	RA	RB	RC
		X		●	X

Item 45 Stress on 't'-bars
Weak or omitted 't'-bars or Stressed 't'-bars/cross strokes

't'-bars are usually formed without conscious thought and as they are lightly attached to the rest of the script they can reveal firm or weak movements of which the writer is unaware.

When the 't'-bars are weak or when the writer has completed or even omitted them the chart should be marked on the left.

Emphasized 't'-bars or other cross-strokes can reveal superfluous firmness in the writing movement even when in the rest of the script the movement is softer. 't'-bar emphasis can take many forms, and should be marked on the right side of the chart.

What to look for
Weak or omitted 't'-bars – left side of chart:
Weak 't'-bars, concave, short or low-placed. Omitted 't'-bars.

't'-bars concave and positioned low

theatre

mkd	mod	sli	sli	mod	mkd
LC	LB	LA	RA	RB	RC
	●				

Three 't'-bars very short and weak, one concave

I'm a sort manager o the but I also do a lot hustli the truck arou

mkd	mod	sli	sli	mod	mkd
LC	LB	LA	RA	RB	RC
X	●		X		

't'-bar omitted from simplified writing

Educatio

mkd	mod	sli	sli	mod	mkd
LC	LB	LA	RA	RB	RC
●					

Stressed 't'-bars – right side of chart:
't'-bars long, clubbed, high, sharply pointed, flying, in lassos, rising, triangular, sword-shaped, convex, heavy with added pressure, twice-crossed. LZ cross-stroke or underline emphasized.

Very long 't'-bar with clublike claw at end

thoroughly

mkd	mod	sli	sli	mod	mkd
LC	LB	LA	RA	RB	RC
					●

Long, high 't'-bars, one with club ending, the other with extra club ending joined on

Herewith the

mkd	mod	sli	sli	mod	mkd
LC	LB	LA	RA	RB	RC
					●

Sharply triangular 't'-bar

to

mkd	mod	sli	sli	mod	mkd
LC	LB	LA	RA	RB	RC
					●

Large, extended 't'-bar forming sword symbol with lasso

Department for

mkd	mod	sli	sli	mod	mkd
LC	LB	LA	RA	RB	RC
					●

Sharp, flying and rising 't'-bars, but pressure slight

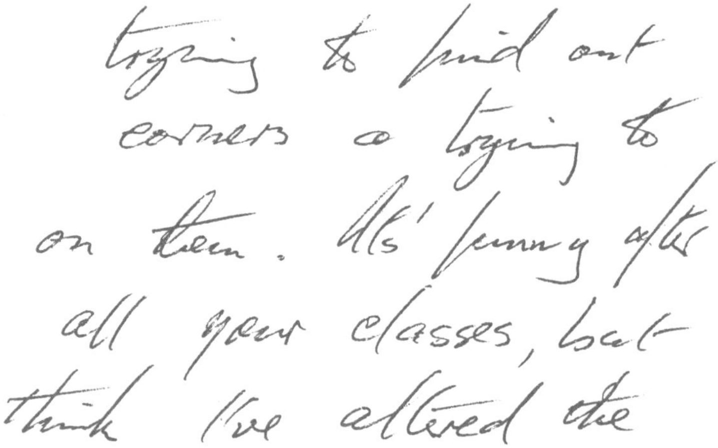

[handwriting sample]

mkd	mod	sli	sli	mod	mkd
LC	LB	LA	RA	RB	RC
					●

't'-bar high above stem, convex
with emphasized pressure

[handwriting sample: "Total"]

mkd	mod	sli	sli	mod	mkd
LC	LB	LA	RA	RB	RC
					●

Unnecessary double-crossing of 't'

[handwriting sample: "Total"]

mkd	mod	sli	sli	mod	mkd
LC	LB	LA	RA	RB	RC
					●

LZ cross-stroke

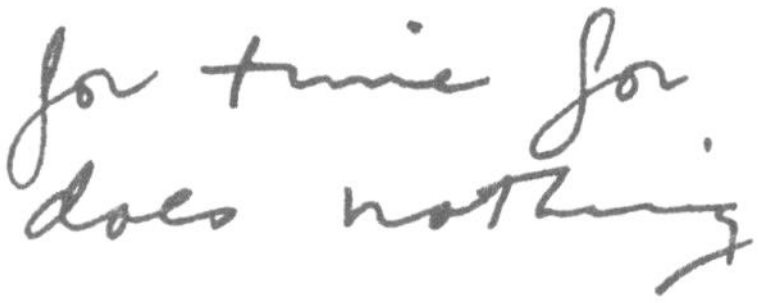

[handwriting sample]

mkd	mod	sli	sli	mod	mkd
LC	LB	LA	RA	RB	RC
				●	

Item 46 Angularity
Soft rounded forms or Angular forms

There are handwritings in which no angles can be found, not even
where they would conventionally be required. These should be
marked on the left side of the chart.

In contrast, a writer whose downstrokes are rigidly straight cannot
connect one stroke to the next except by angles, and the more acute
the angle is the further to the right the mark on the chart should be.
The same rule applies to triangular forms in the letter 't' or in the
place of loops in the Lower Zone. These should be marked right.

Handwritings which are neither really rounded nor angular or
where the angles are blunted should be marked close to the middle
line. Crosses should be used when a handwriting shows both
curves and angles.

What to look for

Soft rounded forms – left side of chart:

Curves replacing angles, uncertain, threadlike or doubly curved forms, circular forms.

Rounded connective forms: no angles even where you would expect them, as in 't'

Item 46

very practicable

mkd	mod	sli	sli	mod	mkd
LC	LB	LA	RA	RB	RC
●					

Uncertain connective forms (ie, not definite connective forms) in quick handwriting

kind – everyone's lives preparing for the and the routine of the

mkd	mod	sli	sli	mod	mkd
LC	LB	LA	RA	RB	RC
	●				

Threadlike garland in hurried handwriting

middle

mkd	mod	sli	sli	mod	mkd
LC	LB	LA	RA	RB	RC
●					

Connective forms in double curves

I am coming

mkd	mod	sli	sli	mod	mkd
LC	LB	LA	RA	RB	RC
●					

Letter forms more circular than is necessary

had an Chau. 9

mkd	mod	sli	sli	mod	mkd
LC	LB	LA	RA	RB	RC
	●				

Angular forms – right side of chart:

Sharp, unnecessary or blunt angles, triangles.

Sharp, blunted and unnecessary angles in irregular handwriting (Napoleon's)

mkd	mod	sli	sli	mod	mkd
LC	LB	LA	RA	RB	RC
			X	●	X

Blunted angles in fairly irregular writing. Final 't' of 'support' written like an 'r'

mkd	mod	sli	sli	mod	mkd
LC	LB	LA	RA	RB	RC
				●	

Triangular forms in UZ and LZ

mkd	mod	sli	sli	mod	mkd
LC	LB	LA	RA	RB	RC
			X	●	X

CATEGORY SIX
50–54 SPONTANEITY

This final category sums up the previous five and is especially related to Items 0–6 and 10–16. It deals with spontaneity and shows how it is expressed in spacing, naturalness, individuality of form and lively rhythm.

When the handwriting is unspontaneous this will show in ornament or complication, in superfluous left-tending movement and in lack of continuity (0–6L). It will also show in stiffness and excessive restraint (10–16L), in impeccable regularity (20–28R marked) and in large curves which are too well-shaped (30–36R + 20–28R). All these features should be marked on the left side of the chart.

Spontaneous handwriting will be reasonably simplified, fast, but not necessarily hurried (0–6R and 10–16R). It will be well-proportioned as a whole, both within the handwriting itself and between the handwriting and the page (balance in 30–36, that is, not consistently extreme on right and left). The form will be free from conventional or fashionable styles and will show rhythmical variability. All these features should be marked on the right side of the chart.

The five items in Category Six are:

50 Adequacy of spacing
51 Proportion in letters
52 Naturalness and speed
53 Individuality of form
54 Rhythm

		mkd	mod	sli	sli	mod	mkd		
		LC	LB	LA	RA	RB	RC		
Inadequate spacing	50							50	Adequate spacing
Letters out of proportion	51							51	Letters in proportion
Slow from any cause (0–16L)	52							52	Natural and fast (0–16R)
Conventional forms	53							53	Individual forms
Stiffness or monotony	54							54	Natural rhythm

Item 50 Adequacy of Spacing
Inadequate spacing or Adequate spacing

This item deals with spacing as a whole, that is, between letters, words and lines, all this together contributing to a pleasant or unpleasant page.

The spacing is inadequate when the writing is too cramped or too wide apart. This applies to letters, words, lines or all of them together, and examples should be marked on the left side of the chart. (NB Compact text on a postcard or aerogram should be marked on the middle line and interpreted with care.)

There are two kinds of adequate spacing, one associated with careful and orderly writing and one with spontaneous writing which shows a rhythmical proportion between the writing and the background page. The mark should be on the right side of the chart in both cases.

What to look for
Inadequate spacing – left side of chart:
Lines and words too cramped or too wide apart.

Lines tightly packed but legible

Item 50

mkd	mod	sli	sli	mod	mkd
LC	LB	LA	RA	RB	RC
	•				

Words adequately spaced but lines too far apart

mkd	mod	sli	sli	mod	mkd
LC	LB	LA	RA	RB	RC
		X	•	X	

68

Words and lines excessively spaced

I   know   quite

and   have   been

there   for   a

mkd	mod	sli	sli	mod	mkd
LC	LB	LA	RA	RB	RC
●					

Adequate spacing – right side of chart:
Spacing between lines and words pleasant in a careful or spontaneous writing.

Adequate spacing in a fairly careful handwriting

fu her notin which wa
fu a beginning but she did
nearly as well as she can.
surprisingly nervous in both
in which she only

mkd	mod	sli	sli	mod	mkd
LC	LB	LA	RA	RB	RC
			●		

Good, clear spacing between letters, words and lines in a spontaneous handwriting

-d card, We would like
rd again next term
idon – it is not very
m us. It's too late
now, so I hope we

mkd	mod	sli	sli	mod	mkd
LC	LB	LA	RA	RB	RC
				●	

Item 51 Proportion in Letters
Letters out of proportion or Letters in proportion

If there is exaggeration in size of zones, whole letters, capitals or particular strokes caused by either affectation or exuberance, the chart should be marked on the left side.

Good proportion in letter size can be achieved either by careful control of the writing movement which may result in some monotony, or it can be spontaneous, in which case there may be some small irregularities which balance each other. The chart should be marked on the right in both cases.

What to look for
Letters out of proportion – left side of chart:

Exaggeration of width or height in any zone. Exaggeration of capitals, of zone extensions. Hyperconnections.

MZ ovals inflated (unusual in a man's handwriting)

mkd	mod	sli	sli	mod	mkd
LC	LB	LA	RA	RB	RC
	●				

Exaggerated 't'-bars, capitals, zone extensions and hyperconnections in spontaneous, impulsive handwriting

mkd	mod	sli	sli	mod	mkd
LC	LB	LA	RA	RB	RC
●					

Exaggerated height in MZ

mkd	mod	sli	sli	mod	mkd
LC	LB	LA	RA	RB	RC
	●				

Effervescent handwriting with oversized UZ

mkd	mod	sli	sli	mod	mkd
LC	LB	LA	RA	RB	RC
●					

70

Spontaneous handwriting with exaggerated LZ

mkd	mod	sli	sli	mod	mkd
LC	LB	LA	RA	RB	RC

Letters in proportion – right side of chart:

Letters and zones in proportion in controlled or spontaneous handwriting.

Good proportion between height and width as well as between zones. Absence of any exaggeration in a quick but very controlled handwriting

mkd	mod	sli	sli	mod	mkd
LC	LB	LA	RA	RB	RC
					●

Fair proportion very valuable because achieved in spite of spontaneous and slightly agitated movement

mkd	mod	sli	sli	mod	mkd
LC	LB	LA	RA	RB	RC
				●	

Item 52 Naturalness and Speed
Slow from any cause (0–16L) or Natural and fast (0–16R)

A natural handwriting is one that is allowed to be spontaneous without conscious artificiality or unconscious straining for effect, both of which slow down the speed of the handwriting. For this reason speed is one of the ways of judging naturalness in a handwriting, and this item is closely related to Items 0–6 and 10–16.

If the handwriting is painstaking or elaborate and left-tending with discontinuity (0–6L), the movement being restrained or faltering (10–16L), then Item 52 should be marked on the left of the chart.

If the handwriting is simplified and right-tending with continuity (0–6R) and if the stroke movement is flexible and certain (10–16R), Item 52 should be marked on the right side of the chart.

However, most fast handwritings contain a few factors of slowness and many slow ones a few factors of speed, while agitated handwritings may contain both in equal amounts. For this reason crosses are often needed in Item 52 and what has been marked in Items 0–16 indicates where the asterisks should be.

What to look for
Slow from any cause (0–16L) – left side of chart:

Slow because painstaking, monotonous, too even, artificial, ornamented, finicky, with left-tending or fragmented movements.

Item 52

Ornamented and artificial

mkd	mod	sli	sli	mod	mkd
LC	LB	LA	RA	RB	RC
●					

Painstaking and monotonous with uncertain, slow movement. Attempt at perfect evenness

mkd	mod	sli	sli	mod	mkd
LC	LB	LA	RA	RB	RC
●					

Certainty of movement but elaborate, finicky and artificial letter forms slow down the speed

mkd	mod	sli	sli	mod	mkd
LC	LB	LA	RA	RB	RC
X	●	X			

Over-knotted vowels in handwriting with certainty of movement

mkd	mod	sli	sli	mod	mkd
LC	LB	LA	RA	RB	RC
X	●	X			

False connections and fragmented letters

mkd	mod	sli	sli	mod	mkd
LC	LB	LA	RA	RB	RC
●					

Natural and fast (0–16R) – right side of chart:

Fast because simplified, flowing, elastic with certainty of movement or animation.

Simplified, fairly flowing, natural

mkd	mod	sli	sli	mod	mkd
LC	LB	LA	RA	RB	RC
				●	

Simplified, certainty of movement, elastic, fairly flowing, fast and natural

mkd	mod	sli	sli	mod	mkd
LC	LB	LA	RA	RB	RC
					●

Simplified, elastic, certainty of movement, animated and very fast

mkd	mod	sli	sli	mod	mkd
LC	LB	LA	RA	RB	RC
					●

Movement very fast in places, but not very simplified and not flowing, mixed with some left-tending movement in MZ

mkd	mod	sli	sli	mod	mkd
LC	LB	LA	RA	RB	RC
		✗	●	✗	

Item 53 Individuality of Forms
Conventional forms or Individual forms

Many writers shape their letters and words according to some
outside standard which can be conventional, aesthetic or
calligraphic. Some even shape them in a special way to show how
original their handwriting is, but in all these cases the concern with
form slows down the writing which should be marked on the left
side of the chart.

In contrast, the writer with 'sentence impulse' who has all his life
been trying to get his message across in the shortest possible time
will have developed his own simplifying strokes and clever
connections to the point that his letter forms could be called
individual. Such handwriting should be marked on the right side
of the chart. Copybook style should be marked on the middle line,
or in RA when it is slightly simplified.

What to look for

Conventional forms – left side of chart:

Artificial, calligraphic, affected, conventional and some copybook forms.

Monotonously artificial and close to copybook

is not good until it is
does not develop its full

Item 53

mkd	mod	sli	sli	mod	mkd
LC	LB	LA	RA	RB	RC
●					

Artificial (calligraphic)

you find something suitable.

mkd	mod	sli	sli	mod	mkd
LC	LB	LA	RA	RB	RC
	●				

A borderline case of affectation in a fairly simplified style: hyperconnection between words and long connected 't'-bar appear contrived in such a disconnected handwriting.

and had a wonderful time –

mkd	mod	sli	sli	mod	mkd
LC	LB	LA	RA	RB	RC
		●			

Conventionally regular with looped connective forms in MZ, certainty of movement but extreme evenness of MZ height

para mim é a casa e
último fim - de-semana

mkd	mod	sli	sli	mod	mkd
LC	LB	LA	RA	RB	RC
	●				

Individual forms – right side of chart:

Individual simplifications from modified copybook to fast, spontaneous individual forms.

Spontaneous movement, simplified letter formation with clever connections and variations

hope you enjoy these
sunning ourselves in Spain

mkd	mod	sli	sli	mod	mkd
LC	LB	LA	RA	RB	RC
				●	

Simplified copybook handwriting with some, but not much, flowing movement

position as
good speeds.

mkd	mod	sli	sli	mod	mkd
LC	LB	LA	RA	RB	RC
			●		

Item 54 Rhythm
Stiffness or monotony or Natural rhythm

The basis of rhythm in handwriting is elastic alternation between
tension and release in the up and down movement and this is often
shown in moderate pressure on the downstroke with some release
on the upstroke.

Handwritings which lack this rhythm are sluggish, monotonous or
overcontrolled with unmodulated pressure and stiff slant. Items
0–6 and 10–16 are likely to be marked on the left of the chart as
rhythm cannot develop without some speed to carry it along. Items
52 and 53 are also likely to be marked on the left as rhythm,
spontaneity and individuality of form go together.

Rhythm is more likely when several but not nall of the items 0–6
and 10–16 are marked on the right of the chart, especially 12R
(modulated pressure) and 14R (flexible slant), and 52R. There will
be some irregularities in a rhythmical handwriting, that is, some of
20–28L, but not so many that the handwriting is crippled, and
these will be balanced by reasonably good spacing (50R). Another
sign that the rhythm is good is when 53 is marked on the right
because individuality of letter form and rhythm both tend to
develop together out of accumulated simplifications of form and
movement driven by 'sentence impulse'.

In the case of agitated handwritings which show a mixture of
rhythmical and unrhythmical movement asterisks should be used.

What to look for
Stiffness or monotony – left side of chart:

Sluggish, elaborate, over-controlled or monotonous, unmodulated
pressure and stiff slant.

Item 54

Sluggish with hardly any
rhythm

mkd	mod	sli	sli	mod	mkd
LC	LB	LA	RA	RB	RC
●					

Too tidy and controlled, reduced movement

mkd	mod	sli	sli	mod	mkd
LC	LB	LA	RA	RB	RC
		●			

75

Rigid. Little difference
between downstroke and
upstroke pressure

Theres' a possibility

mkd	mod	sli	sli	mod	mkd
LC	LB	LA	RA	RB	RC
	●				

Natural rhythm – right side of chart:

Fast or fairly fast, with frequent pressure on downstroke and
release on upstroke, fairly good spacing, flexible slant, some
irregularities and individual forms.

Rhythmical in movement (trizonal) and in pressure and spacing with
spontaneous balance. (The writing of Pophal. See Introduction page 3.)

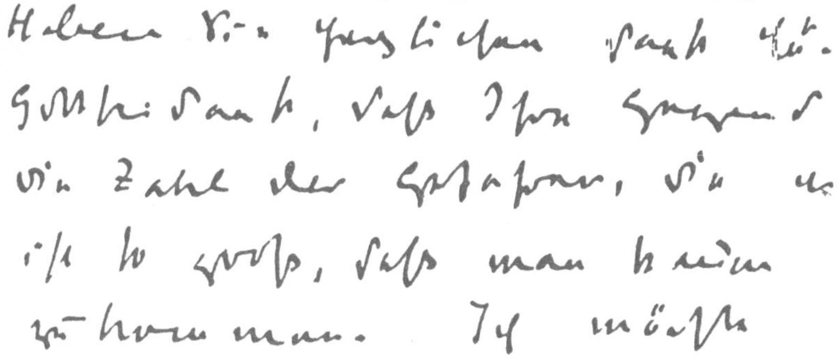

[handwritten German text]

mkd	mod	sli	sli	mod	mkd
LC	LB	LA	RA	RB	RC
					●

Rhythmical trizonal dynamic movement. No attention to letter forms.
Legible though written in haste

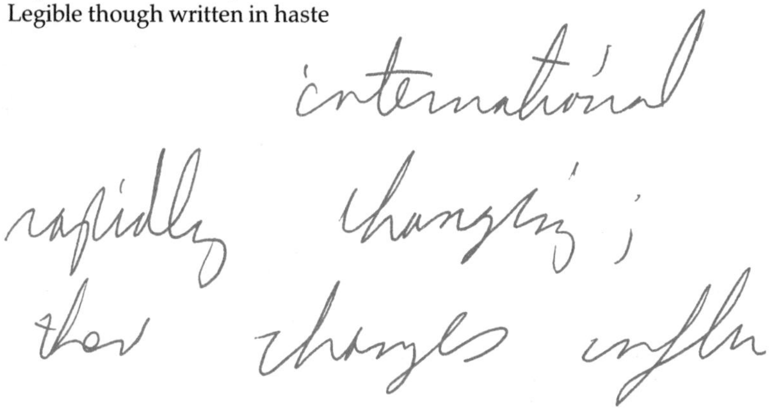

international

rapidly changing;

that changes influ

mkd	mod	sli	sli	mod	mkd
LC	LB	LA	RA	RB	RC
				●	

Rhythmical movement, slightly stylized

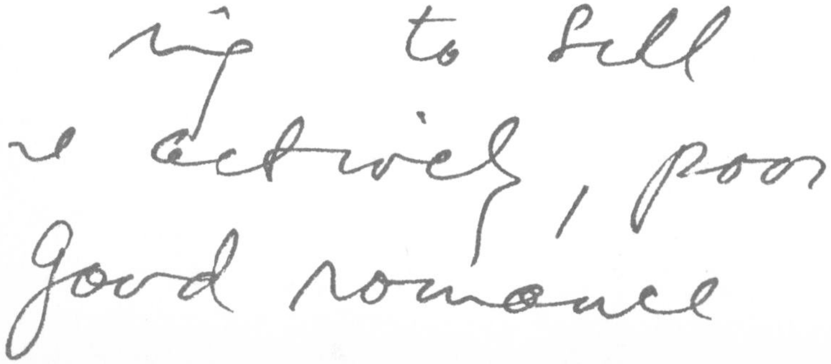

ing to sell

actively, poor

good romance

mkd	mod	sli	sli	mod	mkd
LC	LB	LA	RA	RB	RC
				●	

LEFT-HANDEDNESS

The fact that handwriting is produced by the brain and that the hand (right or left) is only an agent between brain and pen sometimes leads graphologists to consider the question of left-handedness unimportant. However, this should not allow the graphologist to forget all the mechanical difficulties of a left-handed writer:

Difficulties	Results
1 He has to push the pen instead of pulling it.	Less resoluteness of the stroke movement and in conventional letter forms.
2 He cannot see the line because it is hidden by his left hand.	Less resoluteness and straightness in line direction.

A left-handed writer with a strong sentence impulse is more frustrated by these two mechanical difficulties than someone whose writing movement is slower and better crafted (the letter impulse being adopted by choice).

Letter impulse

An old-fashioned graphologist who praises features such as firmness of stroke and orderly layout is not likely to do justice to a left-handed person writing spontaneously.

Other difficulties	Result
3 Very difficult to write with a rightward slant except by tremendous effort or by holding the pen in a special way.	Handwriting either upright or slanted left.

This makes interpretation of the slant in itself rather than the movement that produced it completely invalid.

4 Some left-handed people write their letter 'o' in a clockwise movement (see example, right) and their 't'-bars and underlinings from right to left.

Sentence impulse

Some graphologists have the strange idea that this kind of reversed movement (counterstrokes) can lead to some doubt about the writer's honesty.

The use of the graph will prevent this overemphasis on the signs of handwriting so that the left-handed writer will have as much chance of a fair judgement as the right-handed writer, because syndromes rather than signs are used for the analysis.

SIGNATURES

The signature is an interesting element in handwriting and the lack of it a disadvantage when doing an analysis – though a good analysis can certainly be made when the signature is missing.

When the movement is analysed it will be seen that the signature has much in common with the rest of the letter.

A signature which is elaborated and exaggerated in size is associated with 0–6L, 50–54L and especially 51L. It would be very rare for such signs of exaggerated movement not to be present in the letter as well as the signature.

If a signature is done with an adamantine stroke movement, 40–46R can be expected.

An undersized signature with a hesitating, overrestrained movement tends to be associated with 10–16L and 30–36L.

If a typed business letter ends with a pompous signature full of flourishes, all these basic exaggerations would be present in the letter if it were handwritten.

A simple signature (0–6R) will be hardly different from the handwriting of the rest of the letter which will also be simplified (0–6R).

The signatures of Georges Dumezil (p. 4), Napoleon (p. 5) and Miró (p. 27) contain nothing which is not already present in the handwriting unless a graphologist is inclined to venture into frenzied symbolizing.

In the case of an oversized and ornate signature the writer's conceit and mediocrity, which are beyond question, may require some searching if they are to be found in his or her current handwriting, but they are there.

For reasons easy to understand, examples of such signatures cannot be shown in a book.

GENERAL MEANING OF THE CHART

Before you start the detailed interpretation of your chart, it is a good idea to try to get a rough idea of the main lines of what the interpretation will be. This will be a very rough idea, and if you find it at all difficult (eg if a lot of the graph is near the middle line so that the differences are not too obvious), then pass straight on to the more detailed interpretation beginning on page 90.

These preliminary meanings are the psychological translations of the writing movement dealt with in each category.

General meaning of the chart

Left side of the chart	Right side of the chart
0–6 Slowness – Slow, inhibited, immature or unorganized mental activity. Concern with forms.	**0–6** Speed – Mental activity. Concern with expression.
10–16 Writing movement inhibited, clumsy or rigid – Timidity, anxiety etc.	**10–16** Certainty and flexibility of writing movement – Mental self-confidence, willingness to communicate.
20–28 Irregular writing movement – Emotional, disturbed or spontaneous.	**20–28** Regular writing movement – Either not emotional or very self-controlled.
30–36 Limited writing movement – Expression controlled or blocked, reserved, social introversion.	**30–36** Expanded writing movement – Emotional extroversion, vitality, fantasy.
40–46 Soft writing movement – Easy-going or diplomatic. Sometimes lacking energy.	**40–46** Writing movement firm and sharp – Self-assertion, aggression, competitive extroversion.
50–54 *SUMMARY OF CHART* Unspontaneous. Monotonous or cramped movement causes poor proportion. An artificial, conventional or unresolved person.	**50–54 *SUMMARY OF CHART*** Rhythmic. Freedom of movement with natural rhythm creates spontaneous good proportion. Ability to discriminate and form an idea beyond the facts. Loving qualities.

Rough meanings

The small charts overleaf show rough indications of how the chart will be marked for different personality types. This is only very approximate.

Rough meanings (× shows rough areas where chart will be marked)

Thoughtful introvert

Col 1	Col 2	Range
	X	0–6
		10–16
		20–28
X		30–36
		40–46
	X	50–54

Sociable, overtalkative

Col 1	Col 2	Range
		0–6
		10–16
X		20–28
	X	30–36
		40–46
		50–54

Competitive, aggressive

Col 1	Col 2	Range
		0–6
	X	10–16
		20–28
		30–36
	X	40–46
		50–54

Intuitive, creative, emotionally restless

Col 1	Col 2	Range
	X	0–6
X	X	10–16
X		20–28
X	X	30–36
X	X	40–46
	X	50–54

Orderly, very accurate

Col 1	Col 2	Range
X		0–6
		10–16
	X	20–28
X		30–36
		40–46
X		50–54

Need for affection

Col 1	Col 2	Range
		0–6
		10–16
X		20–28
	X	30–36
X		40–46
		50–54

Vain

Col 1	Col 2	Range
X		0–6
		10–16
	X	20–28
	X	30–36
		40–46
X		50–54

Emotionally chaotic, torn by inner conflict

Col 1	Col 2	Range
X	X	0–6
X	X	10–16
X		20–28
X	X	30–36
X	X	40–46
X	X	50–54

Blocked energy or expression

Col 1	Col 2	Range
X	X	0–6
X		10–16
X	X	20–28
X		30–36
X	X	40–46
X	X	50–54

Impetuous, need for action and social contact

Col 1	Col 2	Range
X	X	0–6
	X	10–16
X		20–28
	X	30–36
	X	40–46
X	X	50–54

Conventional, narcissistic and assertive

Col 1	Col 2	Range
X		0–6
		10–16
	X	20–28
	X	30–36
	X	40–46
X		50–54

The seven stages from chart to portrait

There are seven stages from the first filling-in of the chart to the final portrait:

1 Filling in the chart.
2 Rough interpretation.
3 Detailed interpretation.
4 Gathering the character traits into the three columns 'Mental', 'Inner feelings' and 'Social'.
5 Groups and trial paragraphs.
6 Skeleton plan of portrait.
7 Portrait.

You are now at *Stage Two – rough interpretation* – and from now on a worked example will accompany the text up to and including the final portrait.

The sample handwriting is shown on the next page, and the filled-in chart. The writer is a woman, aged 82, known as 'Jackie'.

Left side of the chart	Right side of the chart
0–6 Self-assertive and impetuous.	**0–6** Intelligent, mentally active and sure of her opinions.
10–16 Some anxiety.	**10–16** Able to get her ideas across.
20–28 Emotional with some ambivalence, conflicts which stimulate her mental activity.	**20–28**
30–36 Not always at ease with her private feeling.	**30–36** Very active socially. Emotions involved in social action.
40–46 Not rigid.	**40–46** Very challenging. Assertive.
50–54 Her exaggerations are products of a strong conflictual personality.	**50–54** Freedom from convention.

I thoroughly enjoyed having your young company. It was such a novelty for me. You were two poor tired souls when you arrived & sat down to your first brandy.

Now I'm going to add a note to your dear mother. I wish she lived in the next street instead of away down South.

We are both too old now to shift about much. In my case I have a peculiar liking for my own bed.

Tell Philippe I received her card & were so happy to bring you both.

Love.
Jackie

CHART

		mkd LC	mod LB	sli LA	sli RA	mod RB	mkd RC		
Emphasized first letters	0							0	Unemphasized first letters
Care of elaboration	1							1	Streamlined simplification
Left tendency: MZ	2							2	Right tendency: MZ
Left tending word endings	3							3	Right tending word endings
Left tendency: LZ	4							4	Right tendency: LZ
Left tendency: UZ	5							5	Right tendency: UZ
Interrupted movement	6							6	Connected movement
Narrowing or neat L margin	10							10	Widening L margin
Descending lines or words	11							11	Rising lines
Unmodulated pressure	12							12	Modulated pressure
Arcade connective forms	13							13	Garlandic connective forms
Slant stiffness	14							14	Slant flexibility
Close downstrokes	15							15	Wide-apart downstrokes
Close-packed letters	16							16	Wide-apart letters
Lines or words unparallel	20							20	Lines and words parallel
Irregular word spacing	21							21	Regular word spacing
Irregular margins	22							22	Regular margins
Irregular 'i'-dots	23							23	Regular 'i'-dots
Irregular slant	24							24	Regular slant
Irregular MZ height	25							25	Regular MZ height
Irregular LZ	26							26	Regular LZ
Disturbed pressure	27							27	Undisturbed pressure
Disturbed curves	28							28	Undisturbed curves
Lean MZ ovals	30							30	Full MZ ovals
Wide right margin	31							31	No right margin
Limited movement (any zone)	32							32	Animated movement (any zone)
Short LZ	33							33	Long LZ
Lean LZ	34							34	Full LZ
Clear interlines	35							35	Overlapping projections
Low 'i'-dots	36							36	High 'i'-dots
Wide space between words	40							40	Narrow space between words
Lines not straight	41							41	Lines straight
Downstroke not straight	42							42	Downstrokes straight
Weak pressure	43							43	Strong pressure
Soft or unfinished endings	44							44	Stress on ending strokes
Weak or omitted 't'-bars	45							45	Stressed 't'-bars/cross-strokes
Soft rounded forms	46							46	Angular forms
Inadequate spacing	50							50	Adequate spacing
Letters out of proportion	51							51	Letters in proportion
Slow from any cause (0–16L)	52							52	Natural and fast (0–16R)
Conventional forms	53							53	Individual forms
Stiffness or monotony	54							54	Natural rhythm

UZ = Upper zone   MZ = Middle zone   LZ = Lower zone

Your chart

Left side of the chart	Right side of the chart
0–6 Intellectual activity inhibited?	**0–6** Or intellect active?
10–16 Timid, anxious, stiff?	**10–16** Mentally self-confident, willing to communicate?
20–28 Emotional?	**20–28** Not emotional, or at least self-controlled?
30–36 Not sociable, prefers to be alone?	**30–36** Sociable, loves meeting people?
40–46 Easy-going or lacking energy?	**40–46** Aggressive, assertive and/or competitive?
50–54 Living within the conventions or unresolved?	**50–54** Balance and/or spontaneity achieved?

Two categories combined

When the chart is moderate or marked to the right or left in the following groups, these interpretations from their combined meanings can help you in your analysis.

0–6L + 10–16L Difficulties or unwillingness in expressing one's feelings, thoughts or opinions spontaneously.

0–6L + 10–16R Flexibility and willingness to communicate with some mental activity.

0–6R + 10–16L Mental activity with lack of communicativeness, flexibility or self-confidence.

0–6R + 10–16R Real mental activity directed to some purpose.

0–6L + 20–28L Tension, emotional problems, inner conflicts.

0–6L + 20–28R Consciousness of self, self-possession and avoidance of emotional involvement.

0–6R + 20–28L Sensitiveness integrated into mental activity.

0–6R + 20–28R Methodical and very organized mental activity. Emotions and feelings are either repressed or suppressed.

0–6L + 30–36L Carefulness or uneasiness of expression for many possible reasons.

0–6L + 30–36R Sentimental extroversion, talkativeness, self-centred impulsiveness.

0–6R + 30–36L Mental activity with emotional and social introversion.

0–6R + 30–36R Social extroversion and talkativeness with mental activity.

0–6L + 40–46L Sensitiveness with depressive attitude. Consistent mental activity is then difficult.

0–6L + 40–46R Rigidity with willpower, tension and tough-mindedness.

0–6R + 40–46L Mental activity with tolerance or with lack of self-confidence.

0–6R + 40–46R Mental energy and willpower. Competitive, aggressive extroversion. Tension with purposefulness (compensating for some inner dissatisfaction).

0–6L + 50–54L The thinking process is impeded by some kind of egotism of self-consciousness.

0–6L + 50–54R These two syndromes are incompatible.

0–6R + 50–54L These two syndromes are incompatible except Item 51 which can be on the LEFT with 0–6R, expressing an impulsive imaginative thinking.

0–6R + 50–54R To the writer, the message was more important than the letter form. The elegance of form, balanced spacing and proportion have more value because spontaneously produced.

10–16L + 20–28L Tension, inner conflicts, blocked energy, lack of flexibility, unhappiness.

10–16L + 20–28R Obsession with details or stereotyped ideas.

10–16R + 20–28L Need and ability to express emotions and feelings.

10–16R + 20–28R Emotions under control with good activity.

10–16L + 30–36L Depression, melancholy and unhappiness.

10–16L + 30–36R Talkativeness out of nervousness, tension, obsession.

10–16R + 30–36L Emotional introversion, but inclination and ability to express thoughts and feelings to someone, especially in writing.

10–16R + 30–36R Social and emotional extroversion. Talkativeness. No difficulties or few difficulties in dealing with people.

10–16L + 40–46L The energy is below the average or blocked or wasted in emotional problems.

10–16L + 40–46R Inner tension, feeling of frustration resulting in aggressiveness, rigidity or intolerance.

10–16R + 40–46L Sociability, tolerance. Flexibility of mind and in behaviour.

10–16R + 40–46R Purposefulness (ambition). Definite in opinion.

10–16L + 50–54L Lack of freedom of expression due to emotional causes or anxiety.

10–16L + 50–54R Refinement with difficulty in adapting due to lack of sense of reality or bad health.

10–16R + 50–54L Pragmatical turn of mind.

10–16R + 50–54R Ability for self-expression and sublimation.

20–28L + 30–36L Sensitiveness and social introversion. Intellectualized emotions.

20–28L + 30–36R Talkativeness, imagination, need for excitement and drama.

20–28R + 30–36L Self-observation. Control of emotion and concern for accuracy.

20–28R + 30–36R Self-confidence and concern for one's self-image.

20–28L + 40–46L Diffidence or flexibility or both together.

20–28L + 40–46R Tension and bad temper. Anger quickly expressed.

20–28R + 40–46L Calm, restfulness. Phlegmatic temperament.

20–28R + 40–46R Self-assertion, bossiness. High opinion of oneself.

20–28L + 50–54L For many possible reasons emotions and mental activity do not work in harmony. Lack of self-knowledge.

20–28L + 50–54R Emotions integrated or at least intellectualized. Productive mental activity.

20–28R + 50–54L Uncritical adhesion to convention or stereotyped convictions.

20–28R + 50–54R Well-organized mental activity.

30–36L + 40–46L Introversion with gentleness, generally diffidence.

30–36L + 40–46R Introversion with inner tension, rigidity and repressed or suppressed feeling. Obstinacy and competitiveness.

30–36R + 40–46L Emotional or social extroversion. Easy-going attitude.

30–36R + 40–46R Natural energy, belligerence and self-assertion.

30–36L + 50–54L Mental activity is either inhibited or subordinated to conventions.

30–36L + 50–54R Introversion with interest in artistic and intellectual matters. Generally critical ability.

30–36R + 50–54L Exaltation, sentimentality, talkativeness.

30–36R + 50–54R Imagination. Artistic or lyrical interests.

40–46L + 50–54L Mental energy either below the average or inconsistent.

40–46L + 50–54R Soft character, either unassertive or diplomatic with intellectual or artistic abilities.

40–46R + 50–54L Tense natural energy with pragmatic attitude and tenacious willpower.

40–46R + 50–54R Natural and mental energy. Willpower and well-organized activity.

One of the main themes of this book is that a graphological feature (such as a pointed 't'-bar) has a different significance depending on which group of movements it is linked with. Here, therefore, you will find each mark on the chart related to other items.

1. Find the mark you made on the chart against the item you wish to interpret. Begin with Item 0.

● For example, on the left side of the sample chart opposite, there is a dot in LB (the symbol for the 'moderate' heading) for Item 0. (Emphasis on first letter).

NB: If the dot is on the middle line, and without crosses, move on to the next item, as there are no distinguishing features to analyse.

2. Now look at Item 0 in the detailed interpretation. If the dot in your chart is on the left side, find the heading for the left side of the chart which in Item 0 is 'Left side of chart: Emphasized first letters'. If the dot in your chart is on the right side, find the heading for the right side of the chart which in Item 0 is 'Right side of chart: Unemphasized first letters'.

   Under each heading is a list of descriptions of different kinds of emphasized or unemphasized first letters together with the marks from other categories in the chart associated with them, and, finally, the character trait or traits they indicate.

● For example, in the sample handwriting in Item 0 the chart is marked LB. Go through the listed descriptions for the left side until you find one that matches it; in this case it is 'Oversized first letter: Capital extra wide including initial stroke with 30–36R, naive self confidence grading to vanity'. Continue to the end of the listed descriptions because there may be more than one applicable, but in the case of this sample in Item 0 this is the only one.

3. When you find a character trait, put stroke marks in the appropriate box on the right-hand side of the page, as shown throughout the 'Detailed Interpretation' that follows this introduction. The number of strokes depends on the positioning of the dot on the chart, see below.

NB: When one or more character traits are given, strokes must be allocated to each character trait individually. For example, in item 35 (Space between interline projections) the sample chart is marked on RC and the description that fits is 'UZ and LZ both long and overlapping with 20–28L and 30–36R'. This gives rise to the characteristics 'agitated extroversion, talkativeness'. 5 strokes (in two distinct groups, one for 'agitated extroversion' and one for 'talkativeness') must be placed in the box, making a total of 10. If, however, the character trait ran 'agitated extroversion and talkativeness' in one phrase, then only 5 strokes would be placed in the box.

Left side of the chart

For a dot in LA (slight): add 1 stroke
For a dot on the line between LA and LB (LAB): add 2 strokes
For a dot in LB (moderate): add 3 strokes
For a dot on the line between LB and LC (LBC): add 4 strokes
For a dot in LC (marked): add 5 strokes
For a dot on the line at the edge of LC: add 6 strokes

Right side of the chart

For a dot in RA (slight): add 1 stroke
For a dot on the line between RA and RB (RAB): add 2 strokes
For a dot in RB (moderate): add 3 strokes
For a dot on the line between RB and RC (RBC): add 4 strokes
For a dot in RC (marked): add 5 strokes
For a dot on the line at the edge of RC: add 6 strokes

4. Crosses

If there are crosses on the left side of the chart as well as the right, treat them as separate marks.

● For example, in Item 2 (Direction of movement in the Middle Zone) on the sample chart, the dot is on the middle line, but the crosses are on LB and RB; you will see on page 92 that both LB and RB are used to find the character traits.

If both crosses are on the left or right side of the chart, use only the dot to find the character trait.

● For example, in Item 43 (Pressure firmness) on the sample chart, the crosses are on RA and RC, but the dot on RB. You will see on page 119 that the dot on RB is used to find the character traits.

If one of the crosses is on the middle line, use the dot should be used to find the character trait.

● For example, in Item 33 (Length of Lower Zone) on the sample chart, one cross is on the middle line and the other on the line between RB and RC (RBC), while the dot is on the line between RA and RB (RAB). You will see on page 113 that the dot on the line between RA and RB (RAB) is used to find the character traits.

General note

This chart is an indication of the writer's character. It is not a railway timetable where if you are very slightly wrong you miss the train. As you collect the character traits you will find contradictions. Don't worry about this: they show the complications of the writer's character. Many crosses on a chart can mean conflicts which enrich the personality.

Handwriting features must nearly always be linked with another section of the chart. For example, the first listing under Item 0 (Emphasis on first letter) specifies 'with 0–6R and 10–16R'). The dot pattern may not always be within those sections, and when this happens put 1 or 2 strokes less.

● For example, in Item 6 (Continuity) on the sample chart, the dot is on RC, but 10–16 is not completely on the right. You will see on page 95 that the characteristics 'discernment, efficiency, intuition and intellectual imagination' have only 3 strokes and not 5 strokes as a result.

The interpretation cannot cover every single feature from every single piece of handwriting. However, any apparent gaps are insignificant. The evidence from the rest of the handwriting will be ample to cover a few uncertainties.

If it is your own handwriting you are analysing, you will find some of the interpretations unflattering, eg 'repressed', 'obsessional', 'self-admiring'. But serious graphology, like psychology, must deal with the deeper parts of the personality where the difficulties that *everyone* has arise.

A glossary of the very few psychological terms used in the interpretation follows.

Glossary of psychological terms used in detailed interpretation

Extrovert/Introvert: An extrovert lives towards the outside world but also has some introversion. An introvert lives according to his own inner world but also has some extroversion.

Inferiority feeling: Conscious feeling that one is worthless compared with other people. An **inferiority complex** on the other hand is unconscious and **compensated** by conscious feelings of superiority.

Narcissism: Inflated self-image with little interest in other people.

Obsession: Need to concentrate on small details to stop forbidden 'filthy' thoughts rising from the unconscious.

Paranoia: Feeling of being persecuted, usually by a person of the same sex (according to Freud, hidden and reversed love). In the wider sense this means unjustified and often competitive feeling of persecution. A strong religious structure is often built on it.

Repression: Unconscious need to keep forbidden thoughts hidden. These are often sexual and incestuous desires from early childhood, mixed with strong aggression. The effort of keeping these unconscious deprives the conscious personality of sexually based energy (libido). **Suppression** is a more conscious hiding of unwelcome thoughts and desires.

Sado-anal character: Unconscious sadism, that is, pleasure in having power over people and seeing them suffer, exercised in a systematic and often benevolent way 'for their own good'. This is called 'anal' because according to Freud it is based on unconscious memories of toilet training.

Schizoid: Emotionally cold, secretive, solitary. Difficulty in forming intimate attachments. Intellect 'split' from emotions.

CATEGORY ONE – SPEED

Item 0: Emphasis on first letter

The first letter, especially the capital, is a symbol of the self, and shows how the writer wants himself or herself to be seen.

Left side of chart: Emphasized first letters

Ornamentation of first letter:

> With 20–28R: social ambition grading to snobbishness.

> With 30–36R: extroversion, self-admiration, coquetry.

> With small ornaments and script: finickiness.

Oversized first letter (This also refers to personal pronoun 'I'):

> Capital extra wide including initial stroke with 30–36R: naive self-confidence grading to vanity.

> Extra high and narrow with 10–16L, 20–28L and 30–36L: inferiority complex with timidity and touchiness.

> Extra high with 40–46R: despotism in compensation for inferiority complex (paranoia).

> Extra high plus thread-like connective forms with 46L: inferiority complex compensated in fantasy about self.

Disconnection of first letter:

> Inner conflict and touchiness when separated from the rest of the word with 10–16L and 20–28L.

> Spontaneity under control when disconnected without gap and with some of 0–6R and 10–16R.

Right side of chart: Unemphasized first letters

> With 0–6R and 10–16R: intellectual activity.

> Chart moderately on right side from 0 to 46, the efficiency is general.

> With 40–46L marked: easy going and negligent.

Draw boxes and fill with stroke marks using the key below:

1 stroke for LA or RA
2 strokes for line LAB or RAB
3 strokes for LB or RB
4 strokes for line LBC or RBC
5 strokes for LC or RC
6 strokes for line edging LC or RC

I I I		

Item 1: Simplification of forms

Left side of chart: Care or elaboration

Painstaking care, conventional copybook writing:

With 10–16L: energy inhibited.

Elaborate, artificial:

With 20–28R and 33R (long LZ): a good employee.

With 20–28R and 2L (rounded left tendency in MZ, looped connective forms etc): insincerity.

Large script: social ambition grading to snobbery.

Letter forms extremely rounded, especially with care for well-shaped forms: self-preoccupation.

With 10–16L: inferiority complex.

Careful and small handwriting (30–36L): meticulousness.

Finicky and complicated: desire to be noticed and care for the details of life.

Elaborate with irregularity (20–28):

With 30–36R (animated movement): sentimentality mixed with repression.

With 40–46R (tense movement and strong pressure): difficult character.

Right side of chart: Signs of speed

Streamlined simplification: General meaning: Mental activity.

With 0–6R and 10–16R: intellectual activity.

Chart mostly on the LEFT from 10–46: lacking in strength and easily fatigued.

Streamlined tendency on syllables and letters rather than the 'sentence impulse' (see introduction):

With 0–6R: aesthetical taste.

Streamlined words mixed with growing ones, so MZ height is uneven:

With 20–28L: emotionality.

With 40–46R: irritability.

With 30–36R and 40–46L: changing moods.

Item 2: Direction of movement in the Middle Zone

Left side of chart: Left tendency: MZ

Looped connections:

> With lack of pressure and disturbed forms (jerks, twists, tremors) this can go with fatigue and bad health.

> With 20–28R, especially *28R* (impeccably shaped curves): extreme social skill.

> Lassos with 10–16R and 30–36R: self-confidence in social contact.

Ovals knotted and closed, or joined twice over:
> Occurring in the letter 'o' only: only a symptom of reserve, cautiousness etc.

I I I	

> When other ovals such as 'a' and 'g' are knotted in the same way the knot is then superfluous and means insincerity.

> Letter 'a' doubled in a bowl-shaped way, with 10–16L: means anxiety and shyness which can lead to a kind of insincerity.

> If a bowl-shaped 'a' is with 20–28R: insincerity with good manners.

> Left-tending triangular connective forms in MZ: stubborn, anxious, tense, with tendency to oppose.

Right side of chart: Right tendency: MZ

No looped connections nor covering strokes, 'n' and 'u' simplified with open stems:

> With 0–6R and 10–16R: intellectual activity, spontaneous sociability and openness.

I I I I I I I I I	

'o' and 'a' ovals open on top:

> With 0–6R and 10–16R: spontaneity, trustfulness, generosity.

> With 40–46L: casualness grading to slackness.

> With 30–36R and 20–28L: unrestrained openness, talkativeness.

I I I I I I	

Item 3: Direction of movement in word endings

Left side of chart: Left-tending word-endings

Word ending stops short:

    With 10–16L: fearfulness.

    With 20–28R and resolute movement: lack of spontaneity associated with willpower.

    With 40–46R and strong pressure: tension.

    With 20–28L and some 30–36R: nervous effort to maintain self-control.

Word ending turns left but is also rounded and directed to the UZ:

    With 20–28R: selfish in a composed way.

    With 30–36R and 20–28L: impulsive, emotional and self-centred.

Word-ending centripetal, ie directed to the writer's body and left-tending:

    Need to hoard and keep, grading to meanness and avarice.

    With clubbed ending: also irritability.

Word ending hooked:

    With a sober and left-tending writing and 0–6L: artfulness.

    If the movement is impetuous, a hook is a simple way to end a word so is not significant.

Right side of chart: Right-tending word-endings

    With 10–16R: amiability.

    With 0–6R and 10–16R: intellectual activity.

The intellectual activity is at its highest when each ending is directed to the next beginning. In this case the last stroke of every line is directed not to the right, but to the first word of the next line.

    With 20–28R: conventional sociability.

    With 0–6R, 10–16R and 20–28L: empathy.

    With 30–36R: social extroversion.

    With 40–46R: competitive, aggressive extroversion.

Item 4: Direction of movement in the Lower Zone.

Left side of chart: Left tendency: LZ

LZ parts are unlooped, fairly short, straight, and not connected to the next letter.

With 0–6R and 30–36L: idealistic introvert.

With 10–16L: anxiety.

With 20–28L: inner conflict.

With 40–46R: bad temper.

Left-tending movement in a graceful curve:

With some 0–6R and a refined script: aesthetical sense.

Also with 10–16R and 30–36R and 54R (rhythm): musical interests likely.

Leftward curve exaggerated and inflated:

When well rounded: hedonism, love of creature comforts.

When misshapen or in large triangles with spasmodic pressure: sexual complexes.

Leftward LZ with an angular or triangular tendency but lean: difficult character:

With 10-16L and 30–36L: repressed personality.

With 20–28L: inner conflict.

With 30–36R, can be childish, moody, demanding.

With 40–46R, aggressiveness grading to harshness.

Complicated reversed movement in LZ with 10–16L: some sexual complexes.

When this complicated reversed movement is oversized (with 33–34R), it can be called 'bizarre': then these sexual complexes are over-compensated by a demanding attitude.

Right side of chart: Right tendency: LZ

With 0–6R and 10–16R: intellectual activity.

With 20–28R: adaptability, both social and practical.

With 20–28L: sensitiveness integrated with mental activity.

With the curve of the graph moderately on the right side from 0 to 46: pragmatical efficiency.

Item 5: Direction of movement in the Upper Zone

Left side of chart: left tendency: UZ

'i'-dots and 't'-bars to the left of the stem, with 10–16L and 30–36L (and usually also 20–28L): anxiety, inhibition, timidity.

'i'-dots replaced by circles: need for personal adornment.

'd' left-tending and unconnected:

With 0–6R and 10–16R ('lyrical d'): artistic taste.

With 20–28L: touchiness.

With 30–36R: subjectivity and tendency to fantasy.

With 20–28R: affectation.

Complicated 't'-bars directed to the left:

With 40–46R, angles acute and pressure strong: indomitable character.

Lassos stretching far to the left with 40–46R: impulsive and demanding.

Looped stems, inflated loops:

With 0–6R and 10–16R, stems moderately looped and graceful, and spontaneous writing: poetical imagination, elegance of mind.

With 30–36R and extremely inflated loops: need to exaggerate, tendency to fantasize.

Right side of chart: Right tendency: UZ

UZ simplified, with 0–6R and 10–16R, 'i'-dots and 't'-bars right-tending, especially if joined to the next letter in a clever connection: intellectual activity.

If also with 51R (good proportion): good judgement.

With 51L: a more romanticizing form of mental activity.

'i'-dots and 't'-bars propelled to the right without any connections, or missing: hastiness.

With 0–6R and 10–16R: intellectual motivation (ie need to get ideas down fast).

With 30–36R: from temperamental impulsiveness.

With 40–46R: from aggressiveness and competitiveness.

Item 6: Continuity

Left side of chart: Interrupted movement

Letters and movement disconnected, even in MZ:

    With 10–16L and 30–36L: anxiety and difficulty in adapting.

    With 20–28L: extreme sensitiveness.

    With 1L (elaborations) plus 20–28R and large letters: need to be ostentatious.

    With 1L (painstaking), 20–28R and small letters: overcareful.

If the connections are false (joined artificially afterwards):

    With 10–16L and 20–28L: anxiety.

    With 20–28R and the false connections look real: insincerity.

If the disconnections go with a fairly fast and rhythmical movement where the pen flies above the page (aerial continuity), this can mean some intuition and originality:

    With 51R, balanced.

    With 51L: erratic.

Right side of chart: Connected movement

Connections mainly between the bases of the MZ letters and solidly done:

    With 20–28R: sense of everyday reality.

    With unostentatious writing: conscientiousness at work.

Connectedness not excessive, but done to a rational degree, eg interrupted to place 'i'-dots or 't'-bars, or inside long words:

    With 20–28R: practical good sense.

    With 0–6R and 10–16R: discernment.

Connections from LZ to MZ, with 0–5R and 10–16R: discernment and efficiency.

Connections from UZ to MZ, plus 0–5R and 10–16R: intuition and intellectual imagination.

Very connected inside each word:

    With 0–5R and 10–16R, trizonal and cursive: intellectual consistency.

    With 20–28R and 53L: unquestioning social adaptation.

    With 10–16L: obsession.

Hyperconnections (between words):

    If with 0–5R and 10–16R: frenzied ideas.

If the letters inside the word are disconnected (voluntary letter impulse) and with 20–28R: affectation.

With 15–16R, 28R, but some of 20–26L, and with rounded irregularity and width: mannerism.

With illegibility but good layout, rounded forms and looped connections in MZ: deceitfulness.

CATEGORY TWO – SPEED FROM CERTAINTY OF MOVEMENT AND FLEXIBILITY

Draw boxes and fill with stroke marks using the key below:

1 stroke for LA or RA
2 strokes for line LAB or RAB
3 strokes for LB or RB
4 strokes for line LBC or RBC
5 strokes for LC or RC
6 strokes for line edging LC or RC

Item 10: Direction of margins

Left side of chart: Narrowing or neat left margin

Narrowing left margin is a sign of lack of spontaneity:

With 10–16L and 20–28L: because of anxiety or fear.

With 0–6L and 20–28R, certainty of movement and roundness: natural ability to keep possessions.

Neat left margin:

With 20–28R: lack of spontaneity, and with 1L (careful writing): anxiety to conform.

This neat left margin is significant if associated with 20–28L, 30–36R, 40–46L and 51L, because then it reveals an unexpected desire to conform.

Right side of chart: Widening left margin

A sign of hasty spontaneity.

When the widening is consistent from top to bottom of the page, impatience in expressing:

With 0–6R and 10–16R: Thoughts and opinions.

With 30–36R: Feeling.

With 40–46R: Anger.

Impatience and lack of self-discipline:

With 40–46L.

When the margin of each successive paragraph begins at the normal place and then widens, the writer has checked his or her spontaneity.

In the case of widening in a serrated way as in 22L: spontaneity with agitation.

Item 11: Direction of lines

Left side of chart: Descending lines or words

NB. If the script is upright (vertical), see whether the writer is not left-handed since left-handedness increases the descending lines tendency as the writer often tilts the page to make the act of writing easier.

Also, a quick reading of the content of the letter is recommended in this case to see whether the descent of the lines is caused by some sad event or temporary fatigue mentioned in the text.

Lines consistently descending and more or less parallel to each other throughout the letter, with 10–16L, 30–36L and 40–46L: depressive attitude.

Lines not consistently descending and uneven, with 20–28L and 30–36R: an emotional and excitable person who was depressed only when writing this letter.

Stepped descending words mean that the writer is conscious of his or her depressive tendency and tries to counteract it.

If there is a faltering tendency along the lines, ie the line cannot be maintained without descending, this means either slackness or fatigue.

Right side of chart: Rising lines

Rising lines straight and parallel with 0–6R and 10–16R: intellectual zest.

  With 20–28R: ambition and self-confidence grading to self-satisfaction.

  With 40–46R: hot-blooded belligerence.

If the lines are rising but not very straight, undulating, convex, concave:

  With 30–36R: cheerfulness.

  With 20–28L: agitation.

When words rise more than the line, the writer tries to check his or her impetuosity.

98

Item 12: Pressure modulation

*Left side of chart: **Unmodulated pressure** (ie no difference between upstroke and downstroke)*

Unmodulated with more pressure than necessary:

    With 0–6 and 10–16 predominantly L: anxiety and lack of flexibility.

    With 0–6 and 10–16 predominantly R: mental activity with tension. | | |

Unmodulated with lack of pressure:

    With 10–16 predominantly L: lack of assertiveness.

    With 10–16R and 20–28L: sensitivity, receptivity.

*Right side of chart: **Modulated pressure** (ie released on upstroke)*

Pressure on downstrokes medium to strong:

    With 0–6R and 10–16R: need to make one's mark in the intellectual field.

    With 20–28R: steadiness.

    With 30–36R: social extroversion.

    With 40–46R: firmness.

Pressure on downstrokes light to medium:

    With 0–6R and 10–16R: intellectual facility.

    With 20–28R and 2L: conventionality grading to insincerity.

    With 20–28L and 30–36R, social extroversion grading to sentimentality. | | |

Item 13: Connective forms

*Left side of chart: **Arcade connective forms***

Arcades clearly arched with covering upstrokes or rising in height:

    With 10–16L and 30–36L: anxiety, prudence, reserve.

    With 20–28R: a wish to keep to the conventional way of life.

    With 20–28R and also 2L (left-tending MZ): secretive behaviour.

Arcades streamlined, in simplified writing:
    With 0–16R and 10–16R: meditative, poetical and introspective.

Right side of chart: Garlandic connective forms

Spontaneous garlands, with no loops or covering upstrokes and with semi-rounded bases and some irregularities:

With 0–6R and 10–16R: amiability and empathy.

With 30–36R: an extroversion full of feeling grading to sentimentality.

Garlands more artificial, with a circular or square base and covering or looped upstrokes:

With 20–28R: ability to adapt skilfully to the conventional world.

With looped garlands as well (2L): secretive behaviour grading to deception.

With MZ also large: desire to be well regarded socially, grading to snobbery.

Halfway between garland and angle:

With 0–6R and 10–16R: intellectual introvert.

With 20–28L: hypersensitive.

With 10–16L and 30–36L: inhibition.

Halfway between garland and thread:

With 0–6R, 10–16R and 20–28L (spontaneous handwriting): intellectual flexibility.

With close-knotted MZ ovals, curved and well-shaped connective strokes with certainty of movement and perfect layout (20–23R): mannered and secretive behaviour.

With 40–46L: unreliable through lack of energy.

Item 14: Slant flexibility

Left side of chart: Slant stiffness

If the handwriting is stiff, especially if upright or slanted leftwards (or even slanted rightwards but very stiff and narrow with arcades): difficulty in understanding other people's point of view.

With curve on left from 2 to 34: suspicion of the outside world.

With high capital letters (0L) and artificial script (1L) and with either a high MZ or long UZ: wish to be more important than other people.

With 20–28R moderate to marked, able to fit into the conventional world.

With 10–16L and lack of pressure despite stiff movement: fear, anxiety, timidity, inferiority feeling.

With 15–16L, 20–28R and 30–36L: someone who keeps his mind closed, grading through prudishness to bigotry.

With 10–16L, strong pressure and 30–36L: most of the writer's personality has been repressed and inhibited.

Stiff slant with good layout (20R and 22R) but disturbed in size, form and pressure (25–28L): anxious, obsessional character.

With 40–46R: obstinate and aloof.

With 40–46R, and slant rigidly parallel with firm downstrokes: an adamantine character.

Right side of chart: Slant flexibility

Either slightly slanted to the right and semi-rounded or rather upright with wide rounded forms and threadlike garlands:

With 0–6R and 10–16R: mental activity.

With 20–28L: sensitiveness.

With 20–28 close to the middle line: social adaptability.

With 30–36R and 20–28L: sentimental impulsiveness.

With some 40–46R, that is, less roundness, more pressure and straight alignment: impetuosity and courage.

Item 15: Width between downstrokes

Left side of chart: Narrow between downstrokes

Downstrokes close together in 'n' and 'u':

With 0–6L and 20–28R: need to hoard.

With 10–16L, 20–28L and 30–36L: timidity and lack of self-confidence.

With 0–6L, 10–16L, 30–36L plus some 40–46R: distrust.

With 0–6R and 30–36L: concentration and reflection.

With 0–6R and 10–16R: some cautiousness in a lively person.

Right side of chart: Wide between downstrokes

Downstrokes far apart in 'n' and 'u':

With 0–6R and 10–16R, intellectual communicativeness.

With 20–28L and 30–36R: the writer's emotionality increases his or her sociability and communicativeness. Talkative.

With 30–36R exaggerated plus 20–28L: impulsiveness, talkativeness, euphoria, sometimes in a superficial way.

With 40–46L: casualness, can be unreliable.

With 40–46R: impulsive audacity and belligerence.

Item 16: Width between letters

Left side of chart: Close-packed letters

Letters close-packed with 0–6L, 10–16L (hesitant, painstaking handwriting), sometimes also narrow (15L) and irregular (20–28L): anxiety, fear, mistrust.

Letters close-packed with full MZ:

With moderate size, ie 51 near the middle line, and a fairly lively and soft stroke movement, that is, not too much of 20–28R and little of 40–46R: warmth and moderate hedonism.

With exaggerated MZ size but fairly soft stroke movement: subjective emotionality.

With MZ ovals horizontally stretched, need for self-esteem.

With artificial forms (0–6L and 20–28R) plus firm certainty of stroke movement (40–46R): narcissism (see Glossary).

Letters occasionally close-packed with 0–6R and 10–16R: some cautiousness in a lively mind.

Right side of chart: Wide between letters

Wide between letters:

Moderate with 0–6R and 10–16R and cursive or aerial connections: intellectual ability.

Marked with 20–28L and 30–36R: a moody extrovert.

With 40–46R and upstrokes straight: belligerence.

With 20–28R marked: affectation.

If the space between letters is occasionally extreme, and the connective stroke is stretched as long as several letters: mannerism.

CATEGORY THREE – REGULARITY

Item 20: Alignment

Left side of chart: Lines or words unparallel

Lines or words now descending now rising:

Draw boxes and fill with stroke marks using the key below:

1 stroke for LA or RA
2 strokes for line LAB or RAB
3 strokes for LB or RB
4 strokes for line LBC or RBC
5 strokes for LC or RC
6 strokes for line edging LC or RC

With 10–16L and 30–36L, words hopping or descending in steps or lines discordant in direction: constant struggle against depression.

With 30–36R, with a lively impulsive movement and sometimes hopping words: the writer is suggestible, demanding, and can be excited by sentimental ideas. Unstable, in need of new excitements, generally over-talkative.

With 40–46L: continuous effort against laziness.

General trend of the lines descending:

With 10–16L and 30–36L: anxiety resulting in permanent irresoluteness.

With 40–46L: irresoluteness due to lack of energy.

With 20–28L: most of the writer's energy is wasted in inner conflict.

With some of 40–46R (especially 43–46R): conflictual, reacting against his own weakness, difficult to live with.

Words stepped and rising, each word rising:

With 30–36L: idealism and weakness.

With 30–36R: impulsiveness and weakness.

Right side of chart: Lines or words parallel

Baselines horizontal and parallel (without use of a guideline):

With 20–28R and 53L: lives in the conventional world, is not romantic about life.

With 20–28R and 40–46R: ambition to succeed in the conventional world, especially at work.

Lines horizontal and parallel but written in a more simplified and faster way than by joining the MZ bases:

With 0–6R and 40–46R: a straightforward rationalism.

Parallel rising lines:

With 0–6R, 10–16R and 42R: motivation, drive and steadiness at work.

Item 21: Regularity of word spacing

Left side of chart: Irregular word spacing

Word spacing irregular:

With 10–16L, 20–28L and 30–36L: anxiety, hypersensitiveness, inner conflicts, difficulty in concentrating and achieving, schizoid character (see Glossary). Still more so if rivers are formed.

With 20–28L, 30–36R and 40–46L: capriciousness, moodiness, instability, inconsistency, easily influenced in a sentimental way; a tendency to dramatize oneself, and talkativeness.

With 40–46L: suggestible and self-indulgent.

Right side of chart: regular word spacing

Word spacing regular in a generally regular writing, with 20–28R and perhaps 0–2L: composure.

When close-packed as well: underlying anxiety. Word spacing fairly regular in a streamlined writing, the lines also being well separated, with 0–6R, 10–16R and 50–54R, and sentence impulse: intellectual activity.

When widely spaced as well intellectual ability and good judgement.

With 32R (animated movement) as well: spontaneous, lively and imaginative.

Item 22: Regularity of margins

Left side of chart: Irregular margins

Left margin irregular:

Undulating in an uncertain way, with 10–16L and 30–36L: irresolute character.

With 20–28L dominant and the left margin often serrated as well as undulating: inconsistency from nervous causes.

With 30–36R: inconsistency from frivolity and capriciousness.

With 40–46L: inconsistency because of casualness.

Right margin very irregular:

Fluctuating confidence in the outside world.

With 10–16R and 30–36R: usually outgoing, sometimes withdrawn.

With 10–16L and 30–36L: usually withdrawn, sometimes outgoing.

Right side of chart: Regular margins

Left margin very neat and regular, with 20–28R: conventionalism.

In handwriting which is irregular (20–28L), unrestrained (30–36R) and casual (40–46L) a regular left margin shows a desire to fit in with external conformity.

In spontaneous fast writing (sentence impulse), ie 0–6R and 10–16R, the writer is adapted to external convention.

Strong sentence impulse (0–6R and 10–16R) can result in the left margin widening in an oblique straight line, without the writer's intention as his or her only concern is the message: absorption in intellectual ideas.

Right margin fairly regular due to conscious care: aesthetical sense.

Item 23: Regularity of 'i'-dots

Left side of chart: Irregular 'i'-dots

Irregularity in position:

    With 0–6R, 10–16R, 20–28L and 30–36R: intuitive thinking.

    With 10–16L, 20–28L and 30–36L: sensitiveness, impressionability.

    With 20–28L and 30–36R: enthusiasm.

    With 20–28R: a corner of the personality is not conventional.

Irregular in form:

    With 0–6R: mental activity.

    With 0–6R, 10–16R and 30–36R: imagination.

    With 40–46R, especially 43R (strong pressure): excitable and aggressive character.

Right side of chart: Regular 'i'-dots

In regular handwriting:

    With 20–28R and 30–36L: attention to detail.

    With 0–6L, 20–28R, 30–36R and 40–46R: conventionalism.

In irregular handwriting:

    With 0–6R, 10–16R and 20–28L: attention to detail in active mind.

    With 10–16L and 20–28L: obsessional character.

Item 24: Regularity of slant

Left side of chart: Irregular slant

Slant of MZ downstrokes fluctuating but not clashing, with 0–6R and 10–16R: the writer's sensitivity stimulates his or her intellect.

> With 20–28L dominant: inner conflicts absorb a great deal of energy.

> With 20–28L and clashing fluctuations affecting the LZ as well: sexual problems.

> With 10–16L and 30–36L dominant: anxiety, fear.

> With 30–36R dominant, with slight pressure and rounded garlandic forms: the writer is lively, adaptable, but capricious.

> With 30–36R and 20–28L both dominant: mood swings.

> With 40–46L dominant: avoidance of responsibility.

> With 40–46R dominant: inner conflicts manifested in belligerence.

Right side of chart: Regular slant

Slant parallel in all zones:

> With 0L (emphasized first letters): need to take self seriously, grading to pride.

> With 2L (left-tending MZ): controlled secretiveness.

> With 2–5L: need to hoard.

> With 1L, 6L (artificial forms) and a high MZ: need to be well regarded socially, grading to snobbery.

> With 20–28R dominant: stability and self-control.

> With a small precise script and 20–28R and 30–36L: ability for technical work.

> With some of 0–6R and 10–16R: rational thinking without romanticism.

> With 10–16L and 30–36L: unconscious repression grading to obsession (the compulsive need to repeat small, unimportant actions).

Slant unvaryingly rightward:

> With 0L (emphasized first letters): ambition and a rather naive self-pride.

> With 20–28R: conventional extroversion.

With 10–16L, 20–28R, 30–36L: unable to move beyond a mundane lifestyle.

With 30–36R: an affectionate nature.

With 40–46R: aggressive, implacable.

Slant unvaryingly leftward: stubbornness, rigidity.

With 14–15L and 30–36L: schizoid tendencies (see Glossary).

With 40–46R: suspicious of persecution (paranoid), and sado-anal (unconsciously cruel in a systematic and often 'benign' way) (see Glossary).

Slant unvaryingly upright:

With 15–16L and 30–36L: firm, cautious in social life.

With 20–28R: cold firmness.

With 41–46R: inflexible willpower.

Item 25: Regularity of Middle Zone height

Left side of chart: Irregular MZ height

MZ height slightly to extremely uneven:
With fairly horizontal baseline:

With 0–6R, 10–16R and 30–36L: rational thinking.

With 0–6L and 10–16L: anxiety.

With 30–36R and 40–46L: casualness.

With 40–46R: rigidity and touchiness.

With letters hopping out of the line:

With 0–6L, 10–16L and 20–28L: hypersensitivity.

With 0–6R and 10–16R: intuition.

With 20–28L, especially 27L: irritable sensitivity.

With 30–36R: cheerfulness and talkativeness.

With 40–46R: aggressiveness and agitation.

Right side of chart: Regular MZ height

MZ height even:

With 20–28R dominant: behaviour stable and consistent.

With 2L (left-tending MZ): ability to be secretive, grading to cunning.

With 30R and soft movement: quiet sociability.

With artificial forms (0–6L and 20–28R) and with 30R, and firm certainty of stroke movement (40–46R): narcissism (see Glossary).

Item 26: Regularity of Lower Zone

Left side of chart: Irregular LZ

Irregularity in the LZ is often seized upon by unskilful graphologists as a sign of sexual disturbance. Occasionally this is the case but more often than not this characteristic may be attributed to other causes.

There are two kinds of LZ irregularity: inconsistent and persistent.

Inconsistent irregularity in LZ size, slant, direction of movement or pressure:

With flexibility, ie stroke movement rounded with slight pressure (10–16R and 30–36R): unrestrained attitude to life, socially adaptable, sometimes sentimental.

With 40–46L: changeable and unreliable.

With 10–16L (tense stroke movement) and 28L (jerks): anxious, unhappy.

With 40–46R, strong pressure and impetuous straight stroke movement producing angular forms: difficult to live with, quarrelsome as well as inwardly conflictual.

Persistent irregularity in LZ may be defined as a particular feature being consistently repeated. Jerks, breaks, twists and spasmodic pressure are considered below. Excluded are inhibited/exaggerated movement (see Items 33 and 34L and R), left-tending movement (see Item 4L) and angularity in LZ (see Item 46R).

The above features occurring in MZ as well and with 10–16L, 20–28L and 30–36L: inhibition, anxiety, tension.

With impetuous straight movement and strong pressure, 20–28L and 43–46R: bad-tempered.

When jerks, breaks, twists or spasmodic pressure occur in the LZ only in contrast with a regular movement in the MZ and UZ, they are significant: either physical handicap (of a non-sexual nature) or sexual difficulties often caused by repression.

Right side of chart: Regular LZ

Regular slender or full loops, or regular without loops:

With 0–6R and 10–16R: mental activity in harmony with social and domestic life.

With 20–28R dominant: social and domestic life go smoothly and rather conventionally.

With 30–36R and loops full but not quite so regular: lively good nature.

Item 27: Pressure disturbance

Left side of chart: Disturbed pressure

Disturbances in pressure often take more than one form, ie pressure on upstroke ('reversed') rather than on downstroke; or on lateral stroke on 't'-bars; spasm on clubbing:

With 0–6L, 10–16L, 20–28L and 30–36L: strong tension and repression.

With 0–6R, some of 10–16L, 20–28L and 30–36L: mental activity with tension.

With 20–28L and 30–36R: excitability with talkative intrusiveness.

With 24–28L and 40–46R: bad temper.

Right side of chart: Undisturbed pressure

Pressure always on downstroke (modulated), even though sometimes on upstroke as well (unmodulated) but not in other places:

With 0–6R, 10–16R and 20–28L, that is, the irregularity that goes with speed, but light and flexible pressure: liveliness of mind with flexibility and adaptability.

With 20–28R: conventional adaptability.

With 20–28R and 30–36L: calm reserve.

With 30–36R: social extroversion without tension.

with 40–46R: severe and aloof.

Item 28: Curve disturbance

Left side of chart: Disturbed curves

Difficulty in forming curves and uncertainty of movement including unintended angles, breaks, jerks and twists can occur in balanced and healthy individuals who happen to be sensitive and tense. When very extreme they can sometimes be a sign of pathology, as can tremors (see below):

With 20–27L, 10–16L and 30–36L: hypersensitiveness, nervousness, anxiety.

With 27L marked (spasmodic pressure) and 43–46R: bitterness, irritability.

||| |||

With 20–28L and 30–36R: agitation, talkativeness.

||| |||

With 20–28L and 40–46L: lack of self-confidence.

Tremors make analysis difficult as they mask other graphological features. They are very frequent in old age but signs of intelligence and other things can still be seen despite them. They occur automatically in the case of Parkinson's or other nervous diseases, the diagnosis of which is beyond the graphologist's capability.

Tremors can also result from intoxication, including alcoholism. Here again it is not the business of the graphologist to make a diagnosis, first because of lack of certainty and secondly for ethical reasons, particularly if the analysis is for job selection.

Right side of chart: Undisturbed curves

Curves impeccable and controlled or still shapely but softer and less regular:

With 2L (left-tending MZ): self-centredness and some cunning.

With 20–27R: ability to adapt to the conventional world.

With 20–28R and some of 40–46R, firm certainty of movement): narcissism (see Glossary).

With some of 13–16R, some of 20–27L and 30–36R: variability and large curves: expansiveness.

CATEGORY FOUR – EXPANSIVENESS OF MOVEMENT

Draw boxes and fill with stroke marks using the key below:

1 stroke for LA or RA
2 strokes for line LAB or RAB
3 strokes for LB or RB
4 strokes for line LBC or RBC
5 strokes for LC or RC
6 strokes for line edging LC or RC

Item 30: Fullness of Middle Zone ovals

Left side of chart: Lean MZ ovals

With 0L (emphasized first letters): inferiority complex compensated in need for importance.

| | | | |

With 0–6R, 10–16R, 20–28L moderate: result of fast writing so not very significant.

With 10–16L and 30–36L: tendency to withdraw from the outside world.

With 0–6R, 30–36L plus thin and clearcut stroke with straight and rigid line direction and invariable slant (14L and 24R and some 40–46R): dry intellectualism.

With 0–6L, 15–16L, 30–36L, 46R (angularity) and 50L (packed words and lines): distrust and need to hoard.

With 20–28L: hypersensitive.

With 40–46R: irritable, aggressive.

With 40–46R plus angularity and rigid slant (14L): stubborn.

Right side of chart: Full MZ ovals

Ovals tending to roundness:

Ovals not over-knotted or slightly open on top in spontaneous simplified handwriting (0–6R and 10–16R) with soft movement (20–28L and 40–46L though not extreme) and freedom from overcarefulness, artificiality or elaboration: loving character.

Wide letters and full MZ ovals not connected but close packed instead (15R and 16L) with undersized UZ and LZ:

Simplified, with soft movement: balanced hedonism with independent but pleasant character. More common in women.

Not simplified, with firm certainty of movement (some of 40–45R) and 20–28R: narcissism (see Glossary).

Inflated MZ ovals with connected letters (6R):

With flowing and animated movement (13–16R and 32R): sociable extrovert.

With uncertain movement and weak pressure: subjective, impressionable and easily hurt.

More or less connected and with painstaking script, that is, 0–6L, 10–16L and 52–54L: the writer has not yet developed freedom to act.

MZ ovals horizontally stretched:

With 20–28L: need for self-esteem from inferiority feeling.

With 20–28R: need for self-esteem leading to affectation and vanity.

Mixture of lean and full MZ ovals in the same handwriting:

With 24–28L: strong emotionality.

With 24–28L and 31–35L: strong emotionality in an introversive way.

With 24–28L and 31–35R: strong emotionality in an extroversive way.

Item 31: Width of right margin

Left side of chart: Wide right margin

Left and right margin in good proportion with the layout similar to a printed page: concern with good presentation.

Wide irregular right margin:

    With 10–16L and 30–36L: fearfulness.

    With 10–16R and 30–36R: restlessness.

Right side of chart: No right margin

No right margin with normal left margin:

    With 11–16R and 30–36: need to communicate socially.

    With 40–46R: aggressive extrovert.

    With 0–6R, 10–16R and 50–54R: spontaneous expressiveness.

Whole page invaded:

    With 10–16R and 30–36R, wide rounded handwriting and certainty of movement: need to make one's presence felt socially.

    With 10–16L and 30–36L, narrow and reduced handwriting with tense movement: anxious hoarding.

    With 13–16R and 40–46L, wide and slack handwriting: lack of restraint.

Item 32: Animation of movement

Left side of chart: Limited movement (any zone)

    With 10–16L and 30–36L: timorous, worried.

    With 20–28L: hypersensitive.

    With 0–6R, 10–16R and 50–54R: lively and discerning intellect.

Right side of chart: Animated movement (any zone)

Animated movement in general always implies some 10–16R:

    With 0–6L, 10–16R and 20–28R, rounded forms and certainty of movement: self-admiration grading to vanity.

    Also with 0–6R, 10–16R, 20–28L and 50–54R: imagination and expressiveness.

    With 10–16R and 30–36R dominant: cheerfulness and exuberance.

    With 30–36R and 40–46R: impetuous aggressiveness.

Animated movement predominantly in UZ:

With 10–16R, 30–36R and inflated loops: fantasy, illusion.

With 10–16R and some 40–46R: ambition.

Soaring strokes and some 10–16R but some 30–36L, light pressure and refined lean letter forms: idealism, mystical tendency.

Large and superfluous lassos in UZ with light pressure: coquetry and sentimental impulsiveness.

Large and superfluous lassos in UZ with strong pressure, and with 10–16R and some 40–46R: demanding bossiness.

Item 33: Length of Lower Zone

Left side of chart: Short LZ

With 6L, 10–16L and 30–36L: anxiety and weakness.

With 20–28L: hypersensitiveness and introversion.

With long UZ: repression with mystical or idealistic exaltation.

With 0–6R, 10–16R, the LZ is short because of hasty movement so is not significant.

With 40–46L and UZ short as well: unassertive, easily influenced.

Right side of chart: Long LZ

With 20–28R: day-to-day realism.

With 30–36R, if at the same time full with smooth and soft stroke: sensuality and hedonism.

With 20–28R and 40–46R: fondness for physical exercise; materialistic and hard-headed in a conventional way.

When the curve is on the left from 0 to 46, and the LZ is long and lean, this can mean repressed sexuality.

With 6R, 12–16R and 34R: social extroversion.

With 10–16L and 20–28L: dissatisfaction.

With asterisks on both sides in 0–6 and 10–16, 20–28L, 30–36R and 40–46R: extreme energy and aggressiveness of a conflictual nature.

Item 34: Fullness of the Lower Zone

Left side of chart: Lean LZ

Looped but lean LZ:

> With 0–6R and 10–16R, LZ connected to MZ without angularity: intellectual adaptability.

> With curve predominantly but moderately on right side of chart from 0 to 45: extroversion in general with adaptability and efficiency.

> With left-tending angularity in LZ (4L and 46R), and 10–16L, 28L and 30–36L: anxious, rigid and touchy.

> With 20–28L: hypersensitive.

Unlooped LZ:

> With 0–6R and 10–16R, and connected to next MZ letter in a v form, the upstroke being slight; or in an 'invisible' way: critical ability.

> With 10–16L and 30–36L: anxious and introverted.

> With 20–28L: hypersensitive.

> Pressure in unlooped LZ increased or spasmodic: bitterness from repression.

Right side of chart: Full LZ

> Moderate fullness, connected to the next MZ letter: sociability and ability to enjoy life.

> If very inflated with spasmodic pressure: sexual excitability.

> With 20–28L sexual complex.

> With 10–16R, 30–36R, a well-rounded and smooth stroke: hedonism.

> With 30R (fullness in MZ as well): self-satisfied, enjoys life.

> Inflated triangles in LZ: see Interpretation for Item 46R.

> LZ projections gracefully curved up towards MZ but not connected: aesthetical taste.

> With 0–6 and 10–16 on both sides, 20–28L, 30–36R and 40–46R: energy, self-assertion and need to show off to compensate for sexual complexes.

Item 35: Space between interline projections

Left side of chart: Clear interlines

Space between lines is clear:

With 0–6R, 10–16R and clear spacing between words: clear thinking.

With 10–16L and 30–36L: fear of chaos.

With 20–28R and 30–36L: need to be accurate.

Right side of chart: Overlapping projections

LZ overlapping handwriting in line below:

With 20–28L: frustration, dissatisfaction.

With 20–28L and 30–36R: agitation.

With 20–28R and 40–46R: down-to-earth pragmatism.

UZ and LZ both long and overlapping:

With 10–16L and 20–28L, the MZ being relatively small: frustrated *amour propre*.

With 20–28L and 30–36R: agitated extroversion, talkativeness.

UZ longer than LZ and overlapping writing in the line above:

With 30–36R and full elated illusory ambition.

With the curve mainly on the left of the chart from 10 to 46, and slight pressure escape into idealism and mysticism.

With 40–46R: dissatisfaction and compensatory ambition.

Item 36: Height of 'i'-dots

Left side of chart: Low 'i'-dots

Just above the stem, neither dashed nor connected:

With 0–6L, 20–28R and 50–54L: part of conventional handwriting, not significant in itself.

With 10–16L and 20–28L: anxious need to be precise.

With 20–28L and 30–36R, ability to be accurate when required by external demands.

Just above the stem but dashed towards the next letter or connected to it:

With 0–6R and 10–16R: ability to connect ideas rationally.

With 40–46R: intellectual belligerence.

Right side of chart: High 'i'-dots

With 0–6R and 10–16R: lively mind.

With 0–6L and 20–28R: conventional optimism.

With 10–16L, 20–28L and 30–36L: hypersensitiveness with idealistic aspirations.

With 30–36R: enthusiasm.

With 10–16L, 20–28R, 30–36L and monotonous regularity: secret idealism.

CATEGORY FIVE – FIRMNESS

Draw boxes and fill with stroke marks using the key below:

1 stroke for LA or RA
2 strokes for line LAB or RAB
3 strokes for LB or RB
4 strokes for line LBC or RBC
5 strokes for LC or RC
6 strokes for line edging LC or RC

Item 40: *Width of word spacing*

Left side of chart: Wide space between words

With wide and rounded handwriting:

With 13–16R, 28R, 30–32R, undisturbed handwriting and certainty of movement: great self-confidence, mannerism.

With 15–16R, 20–28L and 40–46L: lack of stability, lack of firmness.

With narrow handwriting:

With 10–16L: fearfulness.

With 14–16L, 20–28R, 30–36L and 41–46R: lack of spontaneity, coldness, rigidity.

With 20–28L and 40–46R, independence to bad temper.

With large handwriting (narrow or wide), animated or overlapping (30–36R): need for space, offhandedness.

Right side of chart: Narrow space between words

With narrow handwriting and left tendencies, 0–6L and 10–16L: hoarding.

With 0–6R and 10–16R: hasty thinking.

0–6R with lines rigidly straight and parallel (11R, 20R and 41R): obstinacy and lack of detachment.

With wide and animated handwriting (15–16R and 32R): excessive extroversion, lack of detachment.

With 40–46R and firm certainty of movement: aggressiveness, blind activity, and lack of discernment.

Item 41: Straightness of lines

Left side of chart: Lines not straight

Lines convex:

    With 0–6R, some 10–16R and some 20–28L: intellectual or idealistic impulse checked by doubt.

    With 10–16L, some 20–28L and 30–36L: easily discouraged.

    With 10–16R, some 20–28L and 30–36R: unsteady enthusiasm.

    With 40–46L: avoidance of effort.

Lines concave:

    With 20–28L: depressive tendency checked by willpower.

    With 40–46L: lack of energy checked by desire to adapt.

Lines undulating (a more common form of lack of straightness, though more than one kind can occur in handwriting):

    With 0–6R and 10–16R: open to ideas.

    With 10–16L and 30–36L and narrow tense writing: anxious hesitation.

    With 20–28L: inner agitation.

    With 10–16R and 30–36R: vivacity with adaptability.

    With 40–46L: lack of firmness.

    With 2L rounded and 27–28R: opportunistic adaptability.

    Swinging words with 20–28L, 30–36R and 40–46R: excited emotionality, effervescent activity with insubordinate character.

NB: Left-handed people writing spontaneously, ie with sentence impulse, have difficulty in maintaining a straight line. In their case the interpretation should be cautiously considered.

Right side of chart: Lines straight

    With 0–6R, 10–16R and 40–46R: intellectual certitude.

    With 10–16L and 30–36L: unimaginative.

    With 20–28R: steadiness.

    With 30–36L and soft rounded handwriting: calm.

    With 40–46R: inflexibility.

Item 42: Straightness of downstrokes

Left side of chart: Downstrokes not straight

With 0–6R and 10–16R: flexibility of mind.

With 10–16R and 30–36R: social extroversion.

With 20–28L and 30–36R: animation with changing moods.

0–6L and 20–28R: adapted to everyday life.

10–16L: lack of self-confidence.

20–28R and 30–36L: composed and methodical.

20–28L and 40–46L: unsteady character.

Right side of chart: Downstrokes straight

With 20–28R, 40–46R, firm certainty of movement, perfect straightness of what should be straight and impeccable roundness of MZ ovals: narcissism (see Glossary).

14–16L, 20–28R and 40–46R with unvarying angularity: inflexibility, repression, dogmatism, puritanism.

With 10–16L and 40–46R: difficulty in adapting.

With downstrokes firm, straight and prolonged in UZ and LZ but limp in MZ: ambition compensating for dissatisfaction in daily life.

With marked irregularities (20–28L), pressure with effervescence of movement (30–36R and 42–46R), exalted willpower and overactivity out of basic dissatisfaction.

Item 43: Pressure firmness

Left side of chart: Weak pressure

With 10–16L: shyness, lack of confidence.

With 0–6L, 10–16L and 20–28R: individuality not yet developed.

With 0–6R and 10–16R: open, intuitive mind.

With 13–16R, 20–28L and 40–46L: easy-going lifestyle, lack of firmness, unsteadiness.

With 13–16R and 40–46L but some of 0–6R and 20–28R: mannerism.

Right side of chart: Strong pressure

With 40–46R dominant, liking for aggressive power over other people grading to despotism.

`| | |   | | |`

With 0–6L, 20–26R, 28R and 30–35R: realism in a down-to-earth way, instinctual extroversion.

With 0–6R, 10–11R and 13–16R: intellect, strength, energy.

With 10–16L: anxiety and inhibition.

`| |   | |`

With 20–28L, especially 27L (disturbed pressure): irritability, anger.

`| | |   | | |`

Modulated strong pressure with large curves and animation (30–36R): activity with ability to enjoy life.

`| | |`

Item 44: Stress on ending strokes

Left side of chart: Soft or unfinished endings

Soft endings with threadlike tendency:

With 0–6R and 10–16R, some 20–28L and 40–46L, and lines slightly undulating: easy-going with ability for self-expression.

With 10–16L, 20–28L and 40–46L: lack of stamina.

Short unfinished endings with diminishing pressure:

With 0–6R, some 10–16R and 40–46L: intelligent but unassertive.

With 20–28R and rounded forms: calm and reserved.

With 40–46L: easy-going in relationships.

Right side of chart: Stress on ending strokes

Sharp-pointed ending strokes:

With 0–6R, 10–16R, 30–36L and 40–46R: penetrating and challenging intellect.

With 0–6L, 20–28R and 40–46R: aggressiveness expressed in orthodox channels, eg work.

With 20–28L and 40–46R: irascibility.

`| |`

With 30–36R and 40–46R: impulsive aggressiveness.

`| |`

Increased pressure on ending strokes:

With 20–28L, 40–46R and some 30–36R: strong tension, uncontrolled aggressiveness.

`| |   | |`

With 20–28R, 30–36L and 40–46R: strong tension, aggressiveness controlled in normal circumstances.

With 20–28L and narrowness (15–16L): inner tension, obstinacy.

```
| |   | |
```

Clawed ending strokes:

With 12–16L and 43–46R, tense, rigid and narrow handwriting: obstinacy.

With 10–16R and 32R (animated movement): impassioned expressiveness.

Long and straight ending strokes:

With 10–16R and some 30–36R: social directness.

With 14–16L and 40–46R: hostility and resistance.

Item 45: Stress on 't'-bars

Left side of chart: Weak or omitted 't'-bars.

Short without pressure, low-placed, concave, omitted:

With 0–6R and 10–16R: a clear mind that dispenses with unnecessary details and is absorbed in ideas.

With 0–6L and 10–16L: indolence.

With 13–16R, 20–28L and 30–36R: agitated, euphoric, neglects details.

With 13–16R, 20–28L and 40–46L: careless contempt for detail.

't'-bar connected to the next letter at the base with a knot or angle: see 'Clever connections', Item 6R.

Right side of chart: Stressed 't'-bars/cross strokes.

Above the stem, especially if heavy and vault-like (convex):

With firm certainty of movement in MZ (41–45R): despotism.

Contrasting with uncertainty of movement in MZ (10–16L and some 40–46L): aggressive reaction against a feeling of inferiority.

Large left-tending lassos or sword symbols above the MZ:

With 40–46R: imperiously demanding.

```
| | |
```

With 12–16R, 27–28R, 30–36R and some 40–46L: demanding in an impulsive coquettish way.

Twice-crossed:

With 10–16L: compulsive perfectionism in an anxious way.

With 40–46R: compulsive perfectionism with authoritarianism.

Flying (long and rapid):

    With strong pressure, rising and sharply pointed, and most of 40–46R: ambition and competitive aggressiveness.

    With light pressure and horizontal, with 10–16R, 30–36R but some 40–46L: spontaneous nature.

Rising:

    With 20–28L marked: protest as a way of independence-seeking.

    With 30–36R: impulsiveness.

    With 40–46R: ambition, competitive aggressiveness.

Clubbed 't'-bars (increasing pressure):

The meaning is similar to that of clubbed word-endings:

    With 40–46R: certainty of convictions and a desire to impose them. The aggressiveness is generally under control, especially when also with 20–28R, less so with 20–28L.

    With 10–16L and 20–28L obstinacy of a repressed personality, inner tension.

Triangular:

    See Item 46: Angularity.

Directed downwards:

    With 0–6R, 10–16R and 40–46R and sometimes connected to next letter: unromantic concern with efficiency.

    With 10–16L: pessimism, down-to-earth attitude to life.

See also note about left-handedness on page 77.

Crossed underline in LZ:

    Some authoritarianism in private life.

Item 46: Angularity

Left side of chart: Soft, rounded forms

    With 0–6R, 10–16R, some 30–36L and 40–46L: clever but modest, and socially easy-going.

    With 20–28L and 40–46L: lack of firmness, unsteadiness.

    With 20–28R, some 30–36L and 40–46L: calm acceptance of conventional life.

With 0–6L, 10–16R, 30–36R and 40–46R and certainty of movement with width and roundness: self-admiration.

With 10–16L and 40–46L: unassertiveness.

With 0–6L and 20–28R with rounded well-shaped forms and looped garlands but certainty of movement: social skill grading to manipulation.

Right side of chart: Angular forms

With sharp angles, 40–46R, regularity in MZ height (25R) and firm certainty of movement: self-willed.

With stiff slant and narrowness (14–16L), regularity in slant and MZ height (24–25R), 30–36L and 40–46R: dogmatic.

Blunted angularity with 0–6R and some 10–16R: mental activity.

Jerky angularity with irregularities and tension (10–16L and 20–28L): irritable, not very adaptable.

Letter 't' in form of 'v' replacing 't'-bar: dissatisfaction with need to protest. Not aggressive unless the upstroke replacing the 't'-bar is very stressed, and with 40–46R.

Backward triangle in the letter 't':

With 10–16L and 20–28L: touchy, tense and stubborn.

With 40–46R marked: bad-tempered and authoritarian.

Backward triangles in LZ (see also 4L on page 18):

Sharp angles with 40–46R: authoritarian, often in private life.

Large and inflated triangles with 33 and 34R and 46R: frustration of intense primitive emotions leading to self-dramatising and demanding attitudes.

Angular writing in calligraphic style with 20–28R:

This calligraphic style is one of the most frequent as it is relatively easy to learn. It is so artificial that unless it is beginning to break down into the natural handwriting behind it, graphological interpretation is almost impossible.

All one can say is that people who choose to write in this style are often rather nervous and find curves difficult to form. They are frequently connected with the world of painting and can show good aesthetical taste by their choice of this angular calligraphic style which does not have too many flourishes. However, their choice of something so artificial does indicate a lack of self-confidence.

CATEGORY SIX – SPONTANEITY

Draw boxes and fill with stroke marks using the key below:

1 stroke for LA or RA
2 strokes for line LAB or RAB
3 strokes for LB or RB
4 strokes for line LBC or RBC
5 strokes for LC or RC
6 strokes for line edging LC or RC

Item 50: *Adequacy of spacing*

Left side of chart: Inadequate spacing

Words and lines close-packed:

In a postcard or aerogram this is not significant.

With 0–6R and 10–16R: lack of detachment.

With 10–16L and 20–28L: inner tension.

With 15–16L and 30–36L, extreme narrowness and reduced movement: hoarding, anxiety, lack of security.

With 15–16L (narrowness), 30L (lean MZ ovals) and 40–46R: stiffness, resentment, difficulty in social life which can lead to destructive impulses.

Words close-packed, line spacing normal: see Item 40R on page 57.

Lines close-packed but words normally spaced, UZ and LZ projections not oversized:

With 0–6R and 10–16R: ability for non-abstract thinking.

With 0–6L, 10–16L and 20–28R: few interests outside everyday life.

With 30–36R: lack of self-organization.

Lines close-packed or appearing so because of overlapping projections (32–36R): emotional responsiveness.

Words excessively spaced out: see Item 40L on page 57.

Lines excessively far apart: see item 35L on page 53.

Right side of chart: Adequate spacing

With 20–28R: pragmatical ability to plan the future.

With 0–6R, 10–16R, some 20–28L and 30–36L: sound judgement, intuitive lateral thinking.

With 0–6R, 10–16R, some 20–28L and 30–36R: productive artistic imagination.

Item 51: Proportion in letters

This item gathers together the evidence about letter proportion found in previous items.

Left side of chart: Letters out of proportion

'Exaggeration' can be taken as a mark in either LC or RC or on the outside line beyond LC or RC. Note, however, that exaggerations do not always have unfavourable meanings, depending on the context. The item and page references given below are for the interpretation, not the description of the items in the chart.

Exaggeration in:

Emphasis on first letter: see 0L on page 13.

Hyperconnections between words: see 6R on page 21.

Narrowness or width between downstrokes: see 15 on page 30.

Narrowness or width between letters: see 16 on page 31.

Leanness or inflation of MZ ovals: see 30 on page 47.

Restraint or animation of movement: see 32 on page 49.

LZ shortness or length: see 33 on page 51.

LZ leanness or inflation: see 43 on page 60.

Overlapping projections: see 35R on page 53.

Weakness or stress on ending strokes: see 44 on page 62.

Weakness or stress on 't'-bars: see 45 on page 63.

One type of disproportion not dealt with earlier is MZ height:

Exaggerated MZ height, that is, more than 5mm or ¹/₂ inch high: sense of self.

With some of 0–6R, 10–16R, 20–28L, 30–36R and 40–46L: sense of self with outgoing sociability and warmth.

With 0–6L, some of 20–28R with soft, rounded movement, 30R and some of 40–46L: sense of self with amiability.

With strong pressure and effervescent movement (20–28L, 30–36R and 40–46R): headstrong zeal without detachment or consideration of consequences.

With stiff, regular slant (14L and 24R), narrowness (15 and 16L), leanness (30L) and 40–46R: self-willed and unsociable.

With impeccably rounded regular forms and firm certainty of movement (0–6L, 20–28R and 40–46R): class snobbery and narcissism (see Glossary on p. 89).

Right side of chart: Letters in proportion

With 0–6R, 10–16R, 20–28 moderately left and 50R (harmonious spacing): perceptive intellect.

With 20–28R: calmness, moderation.

With 1L (painstaking handwriting), 20–28R, 32L (small handwriting) and 35–36L: very accurate.

With 20–26R, 43R, 46R (angular or semi-angular forms without jerks) and 50R: strong-willed and carefully decisive.

Item 52: Naturalness and speed

Left side of chart: Slow from any cause (0–16L)

Slow writing (0–16L):

With 0–6L and 10–16L, painstaking monotonous movement that is neither simplified nor flexible: lack of skill in writing or fear of expressing oneself intellectually.

With 10–16L and 40–46L, uncertainty of movement: lack of self-confidence.

With 0–6L and especially 1L and 6L, ornaments, left tendency, finickiness and artificiality: excessive concern with appearance.

With 0–6L and 20–28R, especially 25R (evenness in MZ height), exaggerated evenness and orderliness: fear of giving a bad impression.

With 0–6L, especially 6L, interrupted movement, fragmented letters: tension, anxiety, inhibition.

0–6L, some 10–16R and some 30–36R, exaggerated left-tending movement but also certainty of movement and animation, obsessed with one's feelings and opinions.

With 0–6 and 10–16 predominantly on the left, 20–28L and 30–36L: nervous inhibition.

Right side of chart: Natural and fast (0–16R)

Fast natural writing (0–16R):

With 0–6R and 10–16R, simplification and flowing elastic movement: mental activity.

With 10–16R, some 30–36R and 40–46R: self-confidence.

With 10–16R and 30–36R, animated movement: vivacity.

With 40–46R: impatience, belligerence.

With 0–6 and 10–16 on both sides, but mostly on the right, 20–28L, some 30–36R and 40–46R and 51L: extroversion, intensity of life.

```
| I I I I   I I I I |
```

NB: As stated in Item 52 chart description, it is common to have a mixture of signs of slowness (left side of chart) and signs of speed (right side of chart) in this item. The handwriting should be interpreted according to whether the chart from 0–6 and 10–16 is *more* on the left or *more* on the right.

Item 53: Individuality of form

Left side of chart: Conventional forms

With 0–6L, especially 1L, 20–28R, and 30–36L, monotonous copybook style: need to be precise and methodical.

With 1–6L, especially 1L, and 20–28R, especially 28R, artificial, calligraphic, with well-shaped curves: self-control, adaptability and strong need for a pleasant appearance.

With both 6L and 6R and 28R, hyperconnections between words, but within words a mixture of disconnected well-formed letters and some exaggerated connective strokes with long and well-shaped curves: slightly affected behaviour.

With 20–28R, especially 25R, even MZ and firm certainty of movement: self-assertiveness with conventionality grading to snobbery.

With left tendencies (2–4L), stiff slant and narrowness (14–16L), irregularities (20–28L) but impulsive movements (some 30–36R and 40–46R), the forms remaining impersonal: emotional possessiveness and jealousy.

Right side of chart: Individual forms

With 0–6R, 10–16R, 20–28L and 50–54R: emotion involved imaginatively in the thinking process.

With some 0–6R and generally 15R and 16R, simplified copybook with movement slightly flowing: commonsense.

With 0–6R, 20–21R and 30–36L marked in simplified, small and orderly handwriting: objective intellect.

With 0–6R, 10–11R, 30–36L and 40–46R: challenging mind.

With 0–6 and 10–16 on both sides, 20–28L, impulsive movements (30–36R and 40–46R), and unconventional letter forms: ungovernable character.

```
| I I I |
```

Item 54: Rhythm

Left side of chart: Stiffness or monotony

Lack of rhythm is always implied in:

12L, unmodulated pressure.

14L, slant stiffness.

With 0–6L, 15–16L, 42–43L and 46L, reduced up and down movement, feeble pressure and weak forms: sluggishness.

With 0–6L, especially 1L, 10–16L, some 20–28R and 30–36L, reduced movement and careful letter formation: concern with irrelevant details out of anxiety.

With 0–6L, 12–16L and 25R, stiff, painstaking and monotonous with little difference between downstroke and upstroke pressure (unmodulated): individuality not yet developed.

With 0–6L, 10–16L, 20–28L and 30–36L, movement restrained and disturbed: extreme tension and anxiety which cause difficulty in adapting.

With 0–6L, 14–16L, 20–25R and 40–46R, up and down movement rigid and overcontrolled: overassertiveness, inflexibility, lack of understanding of other people.

Right side of chart: Natural rhythm

Natural rhythm is always implied in:

12R, modulated pressure.

14R, slant flexibility.

With 0–5R but Item 6 with some disconnected letter and asterisks, aerial continuity, and 12–16R, 20–28L, 30–36L, 40–46 balanced and 50–53R: intuitive thinking.

With 0–6R (trizonal), 12–16R, 20–28L, 30–36R, some exaggeration of expanse (51L) but 52–53R: liveliness, versatility, ability to cope with informal data.

With 0–6R, 12–16R, supple stroke movement (27 and 28 mostly R), 30–36R and 50–53R: flexibility but also worldly adaptation.

With 0–6R, 12–14R but 15–16 medium, 20–28L, 30–36L, some 40–46R moderate and 50–53R: rational thinking.

With 20–28L, 30–36R, 40–46R, lively impetuous movement with exaggeration of expanse (51L but 52–53R): strong personality who can be difficult.

With 0–6 and 10–16 slightly R, 20–28, 30–36 and 40–46 close to middle line, 50–53 slightly R: adaptable personality.

CHART		mkd LC	mod LB	sli LA	sli RA	mod RB	mkd RC		REF: *Jackie*
Emphasized first letters	0							0	Unemphasized first letters
Care of elaboration	1		X			X		1	Streamlined simplification
Left tendency: MZ	2		X			X		2	Right tendency: MZ
Left tending word endings	3		X		X			3	Right tending word endings
Left tendency: LZ	4			X		X		4	Right tendency: LZ
Left tendency: UZ	5				X		X	5	Right tendency: UZ
Interrupted movement	6							6	Connected movement
Narrowing or neat L margin	10							10	Widening L margin
Descending lines or words	11			X		X		11	Rising lines
Unmodulated pressure	12		X			X		12	Modulated pressure
Arcade connective forms	13							13	Garlandic connective forms
Slant stiffness	14							14	Slant flexibility
Close downstrokes	15							15	Wide-apart downstrokes
Close-packed letters	16		X		X			16	Wide-apart letters
Lines or words unparallel	20							20	Lines and words parallel
Irregular word spacing	21							21	Regular word spacing
Irregular margins	22							22	Regular margins
Irregular 'i'-dots	23							23	Regular 'i'-dots
Irregular slant	24							24	Regular slant
Irregular MZ height	25							25	Regular MZ height
Irregular LZ	26							26	Regular LZ
Disturbed pressure	27							27	Undisturbed pressure
Disturbed curves	28		X		X			28	Undisturbed curves
Lean MZ ovals	30	X					X	30	Full MZ ovals
Wide right margin	31							31	No right margin
Limited movement (any zone)	32			X			X	32	Animated movement (any zone)
Short LZ	33			X		X		33	Long LZ
Lean LZ	34		X				X	34	Full LZ
Clear interlines	35							35	Overlapping projections
Low 'i'-dots	36			X		X		36	High 'i'-dots
Wide space between words	40			X	X			40	Narrow space between words
Lines not straight	41							41	Lines straight
Downstroke not straight	42			X		X		42	Downstrokes straight
Weak pressure	43				X		X	43	Strong pressure
Soft or unfinished endings	44							44	Stress on ending strokes
Weak or omitted 't'-bars	45							45	Stressed 't'-bars/cross-strokes
Soft rounded forms	46			X		X		46	Angular forms
Inadequate spacing	50			X	X			50	Adequate spacing
Letters out of proportion	51	X		X				51	Letters in proportion
Slow from any cause (0–16L)	52		X			X		52	Natural and fast (0–16R)
Conventional forms	53							53	Individual forms
Stiffness or monotony	54							54	Natural rhythm

UZ = Upper zone   MZ = Middle zone   LZ = Lower zone

Stage Four Gathering the character traits into three columns which are always marked 'Mental', 'Inner feelings' and 'Social'

Go through your detailed interpretation and put each character trait with its appropriate number of strokes into one or more of these columns. (For example, 'emotionality' could be in both 'Inner feelings' and 'Social'.)

When you find a character trait you have already used (eg 'mental activity') add the strokes to it but do not repeat it.

The order of the character traits within each column does not matter, but it is a good idea to leave enough space round the first traits you enter so that you can place similar ones near it, eg 'aggressiveness' next to 'agitated aggressiveness'.

As you fill in the columns you may simplify the traits a little – for example, 'mental activity' and 'intellectual activity' can be amalgamated, not forgetting to amalgamate their strokes as well.

The worked example below shows how Jackie's character traits (marked in blue in the detailed interpretation) are gathered into these three columns.

Stage Five Groups and trial paragraphs

Group the character traits within their columns and then make them into trial paragraphs

The character traits are always divided into the same three *columns*, 'Mental', 'Inner feelings' and 'Social', but the *groups* within the columns are entirely up to you. Division into groups makes the analysis much easier to deal with, but the subject of each group and the number of groups are your choice. For instance, in the worked example, Jackie's 'Mental' traits fall roughly into five groups:

1 Mental activity.
2 Speed of thinking.
3 Different ways of thinking.
4 The effect of her thinking on the outside world.
5 Its connection with her inner feelings.

But the groups in another handwriting might be quite different: perhaps a group of logical thoughts and another of confused thoughts, perhaps two groups, perhaps ten.

The order of the groups does not matter, but it is a good idea to start with a group of traits which have several strokes.

Put a trait in brackets when you have already used it in one group but feel it also fits in another.

To continue with the worked example, Jackie's 'Mental' column will now be put into groups, then into trial paragraphs.

In the group stage keep the strokes so that you can judge the relative importance of each trait.

Column: Mental

Group 1: Mental activity

mental activity III III III III I

Trial paragraph

Her mind is extremely active.

Group 2: Speed of thinking

hastiness with intellectual
   motivation I
frenzied ideas I
impatience in expressing thoughts
   and opinions I
hasty thinking II
some cautiousness in a lively
   mind III

Her thought processes are very quick, in fact too quick. Ideas whirl about in her mind in a frenzy, she is impatient to express her thoughts and opinions and does so in haste; though occasionally she stops to consider with some caution.

Group 3: Different ways of thinking

romantizing form of mental activity
   II
discernment II
lack of discernment II
lack of detachment II
intuition III II
imagination III
imaginative expressiveness III
some productive artistic
   imagination II
intellectual ability I
some ability to cope with informal
   data I
some versatility I
lively mind II

As this is a large group of traits it will be easier to handle if subdivided into:

1 Romantic thinking versus discernment.
2 Intuition and imagination.
3 Intellectual ability.

Romantic thinking versus discernment:

Her thoughts are coloured with romanticism and because this hampers her objectivity it interferes frequently – but not always – with her powers of discernment. Sometimes, however, shrewd criticism wins through.

Intuition and imagination:
She thinks intuitively and has some imagination which can occasionally take the form of artistic expression.

Intellectual ability:
She has a lively mind and enough intellectual ability and versatility to see the matching parts in seemingly disparate ideas.

Group 4: Effect of her thinking on the outside world

certainty of convictions and desire to impose them III III

intellectual introvert I

protest as a way of independence-seeking III III

She is certain that her ideas are right and is determined to impose them.

These ideas are often protests against the way things are; they are reforming and political and her efforts to get them across reassure her that she is independent of constraints.

(Her protests would be reforming and political because she lives very much in an extrovert world and protests and is convinced she is right.)

Group 5: Connection with her inner feelings

sensitiveness integrated with mental activity I

sensitivity stimulates intellect III

mental activity with tension I

The frenzied speed of her ideas and constant need to get them across are stimulated by inner tension and sensitivity.

Inner feelings

Group 1: Sensitivity

hypersensitive III III III

sensitive III

irritable sensitivity III II

Group 2: Irritability

irritability III III

Group 3: Tension, anxiety, inner conflict

tense and nervous effort to maintain self-control II

strong tensions II

inner tension I

nervous inhibition II

inhibition II

anxiety II

inner conflict absorbs a lot of energy I

inner conflict III

aggressiveness of a conflictual nature I

Group 4: Aggression

hot-blooded belligerence III

(aggressiveness of a conflictual nature I

aggressiveness and agitation III II

Group 5: Agitation

agitation III III

(aggressiveness and agitation III II)

Group 6: Bitterness and depression

bitterness III

bitterness from repression III

depressive tendency the writer tries to counteract (perhaps partly due to old age) I

Group 7: Enjoyment of life

cheerfulness III III II

enthusiastic IIII

activity with the ability to enjoy life III

intensity of life III I

liveliness I

love of creature comforts I

Group 8: Energy

extreme energy II

energy and need to show off III II

Group 9: Excitement

needs new excitements II

suggestible II

Group 10: Impulsiveness and impatience

hastiness from temperamental impulsiveness II

impatience in expressing feeling I

impatience in expressing anger I

impulsiveness III III

Group 11: Cautiousness

cautiousness III

cautiousness in a lively person III III

Group 12: Emotion

strong emotionality in an extroversive way **III II**

excited emotionality **III**

extroversion full of feeling grading to sentimentality **I**

emotional responsiveness **II**

warmth **III**

mood swings **I**

Group 13: Sentimentality

sentimentality mixed with repression **II**

(extroversion full of feeling grading to sentimentality **I**)

excited by sentimental ideas **II**

Group 14: Dissatisfaction, compensation and ambition

ambition **III III III III**

exalted willpower **II**

and overactivity **II**

out of basic dissatisfaction **II**

self-assertion to compensate for sexual complexes **III II**

inferiority complex compensated in need for importance **III II**

naive self-confidence grading to vanity **II**

Group 15: Independence

independence of character **II**

grading to bad temper **II**

need for space **II**

sense of self **I**

protest as a way of independence-seeking **III III**

Social

Group 1: Difficult and independent

difficult character **II**

difficult to live with **III**

independence of character **II**

grading to bad temper **II**

insubordinate character **III I**

ungovernable character **III**

strong personality who can be difficult **III**

protest as a way of independence-seeking **III III**

obstinacy of a repressed personality **III**

efficiency **III**

Group 2: Aggressiveness

bad temper **II**

quarrelsome **III**

irritability **III III III I**

extreme energy and aggressiveness of a conflictual nature **II**

impulsive aggressiveness **II**

uncontrolled aggressiveness **II**

impetuous aggressiveness **III**

aggressive extroversion **II**

aggressiveness and agitation **III II**

inner conflict manifested in belligerence **I**

competitive aggressiveness **III III III III I**

aggressive **III II**

hastiness from competitive aggressiveness **III**

hot-blooded belligerence **III**

impatience in expressing anger **I**

aggressiveness not really under control **III III**

Group 3: Power over people

liking for aggressive power over other people **III**

despotism **III**

certainty of convictions and a desire to impose them **III III**

imperiously demanding **IIIII**

offhand **II**

Group 4: Impulsiveness and enthusiasm

enthusiasm **IIII**

headstrong zeal without detachment or consideration of consequences **II**

sentimental impulsiveness **III**

impatience in expressing anger **I**

impatience in expressing thoughts and opinions **I**

impatience in expressing feelings **I**

unrestrained openness **III**

Group 5: Extroversion and sociability

spontaneous sociability **III**

social extroversion **III III III III I**

talkative **III III III III III**

excitability and intrusive talkativeness **II**

extroversion full of feeling grading to sentimentality **I**

need to communicate socially **II**

agitated extroversion **III II**

excessive extroversion **II**

(aggressive extroversion **II**

)empathy **II**

demanding **II**

Group 6: Emotionality and moods

cheerfulness **III III III II**

exuberance **III**

amiability **II**

strong emotionality in an extroversive way **III II**

emotional responsiveness **II**

warmth **III**

moody extrovert **I**

mood swings **I**

inconsistency from nervous causes **I**

inconsistency from frivolity and capriciousness **I**

unstable **II**

spontaneity **III**

openness **III**

Stage Six Skeleton plan of portrait

The next stage is to make a plan for the portrait.

The key to this is to choose which of the three columns ('Mental', 'Inner feelings' or 'Social') is the most important in the character you are analysing. In the case of the worked example, 'Social' is the most important and 'Inner feelings' shows why she behaves as she does in both 'Social' and 'Mental' fields.

This order of the three columns is the basis of your plan. You now need an introduction and conclusion.

For the introduction it is a good idea to pull back from your detailed work and ask yourself what is the most striking impression you get from this handwriting. In Jackie's case it is her vitality, especially when you consider her age.

For the conclusion you recapitulate this, relate it to love and work and suggest what is most difficult and most hopeful for the character you are analysing.

At this stage you may use your knowledge of psychology but be careful to restrain unfounded intuition.

Finally, write it as if the person who did the handwriting is going to read it.

GRAPHOLOGICAL PORTRAIT Woman 82

The most striking impression from this handwriting is one of vitality and still more so when the writer's age (82) is considered.

Above all she is an extrovert: an enormous amount of her terrific energy goes into exuberant or belligerent contact with people. She is spontaneously sociable, she talks and talks whether or not people want to listen, and lets out her strong, impetuous and changeable emotions. She is often cheerful, can be amiable, empathic and responsive, though sometimes sentimental; then she is capricious, inconsistent; then quarrelsome, full of hot-blooded belligerence, aggressive in a very competitive way and ready to rush into confrontations. Her aggression can come in sudden storms but there is also in her a more lasting state of irritability, obstinacy and a competitive need for power over people. She is certain that she is right and can be imperiously despotic. She is what is called a difficult character, not easy to live or work with, insubordinate, independent and full of protest – and yet she is also stimulating, full of vitality and human.

Her mind is very active, so that she is often in a frenzy of thought. She comes to hasty conclusions, usually on a romantic rather than a factual basis, and pours out her ideas without stopping to consider. She has some imagination, intuition and ability to express herself, though this is usually in the form of speech. She has some intellectual ability with versatility and powers of discernment and even caution but she does not often allow herself time to use them.

It is at first surprising to find that such an energetic, belligerent and extroverted person is in her inner feelings very sensitive. She has some conscious bitterness but her sensitivity shows itself most often unconsciously in the form of frequent irritability. The constant tension of her conscious efforts of control makes her anxious and inhibited and absorbs a great deal of her abundant natural energy. At the core of her life was something in the past that made emotional and sexual satisfaction not easy to come by, that made her emotions ambivalent and gave her a desperate need to seem important. This need, though it wastes much of her energy, also stimulates a great deal more energy, though this has an anxious, overactive tone. She is extremely ambitious, needs to assert herself, and is full of exalted willpower.

This energy, partly stimulated by her inner tension, also shows itself in her happier moods: she brims with cheerfulness, enthusiasm and a feeling of being intensely alive. She rushes about, chases new excitements, responds to new ideas (and new forms of protest) and even shows off. She enjoys her creature comforts and relishes living a full and active life.

Her life of emotional relationships is difficult. She has strong emotions towards people, though these are marred a little by sentimentality arising from her repression; but she also needs to be in the right and to dominate, and her need for independence and need to protest make it impossible for her to accept any compromise. These qualities could, however, be fruitful in a ruthlessly honest, perhaps sexually rather distant relationship that involved some mutual campaigns of social protest.

In her life of work she would not last long as an employee unless she believed passionately in what she was doing, and even then she would have difficulties with her bosses. But in a situation where she could act independently, such as some form of political or social campaigning, she would be a tremendously active fighter and speaker, and even reasonably efficient. Her liking for command over people could make her protective of her subordinates, and she would sometimes show some empathy – but not always.

She needs social activities not only because of her energetic temperament but also as a way of overcoming her sensitivity.

COMPATIBILITY

Graphologists are usually consulted in one of two situations: first, when someone has advertised in the lonely hearts column of a magazine and has received several replies; secondly, difficulties have appeared in a relationship which has lasted several months or years.

There are cases where incompatibility is obvious to a well-trained graphologist. Compatibility, on the other hand, is never as definite: even the best prognosis does not exclude some need for adjustment.

Compatibility study (sample). Man aged 42: woman aged 39

These two met through a dating agency, and the prospects for the relationship looked good:

- He was 42. She was 39.
- Both were handsome. He was slightly taller and slimmer.
- Both came from a similar background.
- Both were graduates.
- The similarity of their interests was remarkable; both were interested in psychology, both liked classical music, especially Wagner, and they had similar political ideals.

They were naturally attracted to each other (especially him to her).

- He was fascinated by her self-confidence in social contacts, her ability to talk, her liveliness of manner, her enthusiasm.
- She at first considered his obvious tension as a sign of deep intellect which was something she thought she lacked.

Their first two meetings were rather impersonal without real conversation: concert, opera.

Their third meeting was in a restaurant with, of course, a long conversation which became emotional. She found him pedantic and not at all as deep as she had suspected, but rather narrow-minded. He was frightened by her easy expansiveness but (because of the law of contrast) more in love.

As a result she quickly saw him as more gloomy than deep. She was less willing to meet him again. This made him possessive and his aggressive tendencies began to surface.

CHART		mkd LC	mod LB	sli LA	sli RA	mod RB	mkd RC		REF: woman 39
Emphasized first letters	0							0	Unemphasized first letters
Care of elaboration	1			X			X	1	Streamlined simplification
Left tendency: MZ	2		X				X	2	Right tendency: MZ
Left tending word endings	3			X			X	3	Right tending word endings
Left tendency: LZ	4			X		X		4	Right tendency: LZ
Left tendency: UZ	5		X		X			5	Right tendency: UZ
Interrupted movement	6							6	Connected movement
Narrowing or neat L margin	10							10	Widening L margin
Descending lines or words	11							11	Rising lines
Unmodulated pressure	12							12	Modulated pressure
Arcade connective forms	13							13	Garlandic connective forms
Slant stiffness	14							14	Slant flexibility
Close downstrokes	15			X			X	15	Wide-apart downstrokes
Close-packed letters	16							16	Wide-apart letters
Lines or words unparallel	20							20	Lines and words parallel
Irregular word spacing	21							21	Regular word spacing
Irregular margins	22							22	Regular margins
Irregular 'i'-dots	23							23	Regular 'i'-dots
Irregular slant	24							24	Regular slant
Irregular MZ height	25							25	Regular MZ height
Irregular LZ	26							26	Regular LZ
Disturbed pressure	27							27	Undisturbed pressure
Disturbed curves	28		X				X	28	Undisturbed curves
Lean MZ ovals	30			X			X	30	Full MZ ovals
Wide right margin	31							31	No right margin
Limited movement (any zone)	32				X		X	32	Animated movement (any zone)
Short LZ	33			X			X	33	Long LZ
Lean LZ	34			X			X	34	Full LZ
Clear interlines	35							35	Overlapping projections
Low 'i'-dots	36			X			X	36	High 'i'-dots
Wide space between words	40	X		X				40	Narrow space between words
Lines not straight	41							41	Lines straight
Downstroke not straight	42							42	Downstrokes straight
Weak pressure	43							43	Strong pressure
Soft or unfinished endings	44							44	Stress on ending strokes
Weak or omitted 't'-bars	45			X			X	45	Stressed 't'-bars/cross-strokes
Soft rounded forms	46							46	Angular forms
Inadequate spacing	50							50	Adequate spacing
Letters out of proportion	51							51	Letters in proportion
Slow from any cause (0–16L)	52							52	Natural and fast (0–16R)
Conventional forms	53							53	Individual forms
Stiffness or monotony	54							54	Natural rhythm

UZ = Upper zone   MZ = Middle zone   LZ = Lower zone

Hubert Desenclos Copyright © 1990

Woman 39

Mental

intellectual activity ||||| |||||
sensitiveness integrated with
    mental activity ||
romantic form of mental activity |
intellectual frenzy ||||| |
intellectual expansiveness |
intellectual zest |||
intellectual flexibility ||
empathy |
intellectual communicativeness |
unpredictable ideas |
intellect stimulated by
    sensitivity |||
intellectual adaptability ||
imagination ||||
gracefulness ||||
exalted imagination ||||
lively mind ||
consistent mental energy |
intellectual purposefulness ||
lack of self-organization |||
mental activity, but the intellectual
    ambitions are limited, she rather
    has practical pragmatic
    ambitions, ie success |||
mental activity associated with
    social extroversion ||||| |
imagination with ability for self-
    expression ||||| |

Inner feelings

emotionality ||||| |||
narcissism |||
hypersensitiveness |||||
emotional waste of energy ||||
emotional ambivalence |
nervousness |||
self-admiration mixed with
    sensitiveness and
    impressionability ||||
feeling of success ||||
erratic emotional attitude ||||
self-admiration grading to
    vanity ||||
sexual complexes ||
hedonism ||
illusion |||
egocentric |||
inner conflicts and emotional
    problems stimulate her
    mind ||||| |

Social

changing mood ||||| ||||
self-confidence in social contact |||
talkativeness ||||| ||||| ||
amiability ||||| ||
social extroversion ||||| ||||| ||||
tendency to fantasize |||
some mannerisms ||||| |
emotional expansiveness |
cheerfulness ||||| ||
agitation ||||| |
adaptability ||
sentimentality |||
emotional impulsiveness grading to
    sentimental impulsiveness ||||| |
the writer's emotionality increases
    her sociability and
    communicativeness and
    talkativeness ||||
tendency to dramatize herself |
desire to cope with external
    reality |||||
adaptability to external
    convention ||||| ||
lively, adaptable but capricious |||
erratic ||
open feeling, rather sentimental
    and superficial |||
unrestrained attitude to life,
    sometimes sentimental but
    socially adaptable |||
liveliness in rather superficial
    way ||
need of space, offhandedness ||
impulsiveness ||
obstinacy ||
pleasure seeker |||
cordiality |||
sociability |||
has more cleverness than
    principles |||

CHART		mkd LC	mod LB	sli LA	sli RA	mod RB	mkd RC	REF: man 42	
Emphasized first letters	0		X	●	X			0	Unemphasized first letters
Care of elaboration	1		X	●	X			1	Streamlined simplification
Left tendency: MZ	2		X	●	X			2	Right tendency: MZ
Left tending word endings	3			●				3	Right tending word endings
Left tendency: LZ	4			●				4	Right tendency: LZ
Left tendency: UZ	5		X	●	X			5	Right tendency: UZ
Interrupted movement	6					●		6	Connected movement
Narrowing or neat L margin	10			●				10	Widening L margin
Descending lines or words	11		X	●		X		11	Rising lines
Unmodulated pressure	12			●				12	Modulated pressure
Arcade connective forms	13		●					13	Garlandic connective forms
Slant stiffness	14		●					14	Slant flexibility
Close downstrokes	15	X	●	X				15	Wide-apart downstrokes
Close-packed letters	16			●				16	Wide-apart letters
Lines or words unparallel	20		●					20	Lines and words parallel
Irregular word spacing	21		●					21	Regular word spacing
Irregular margins	22			●				22	Regular margins
Irregular 'i'-dots	23			●				23	Regular 'i'-dots
Irregular slant	24	●						24	Regular slant
Irregular MZ height	25		●					25	Regular MZ height
Irregular LZ	26		●					26	Regular LZ
Disturbed pressure	27			●				27	Undisturbed pressure
Disturbed curves	28		X	●	X			28	Undisturbed curves
Lean MZ ovals	30			●				30	Full MZ ovals
Wide right margin	31			●				31	No right margin
Limited movement (any zone)	32		X	●	X			32	Animated movement (any zone)
Short LZ	33			X	●	X		33	Long LZ
Lean LZ	34		X	●	X			34	Full LZ
Clear interlines	35				●			35	Overlapping projections
Low 'i'-dots	36			X	●	X		36	High 'i'-dots
Wide space between words	40				X	●	X	40	Narrow space between words
Lines not straight	41		●					41	Lines straight
Downstroke not straight	42		●					42	Downstrokes straight
Weak pressure	43			X	●	X		43	Strong pressure
Soft or unfinished endings	44		X		●	X		44	Stress on ending strokes
Weak or omitted 't'-bars	45					●		45	Stressed 't'-bars/cross-strokes
Soft rounded forms	46				●			46	Angular forms
Inadequate spacing	50		●					50	Adequate spacing
Letters out of proportion	51			●				51	Letters in proportion
Slow from any cause (0–16L)	52		X	●	X			52	Natural and fast (0–16R)
Conventional forms	53			●				53	Individual forms
Stiffness or monotony	54			●				54	Natural rhythm

UZ = Upper zone   MZ = Middle zone   LZ = Lower zone

Man 42

Mental

cautiousness I

pedantry and fussiness II

Inner feelings

attempt to compensate for
inferiority complex IIII

blockage of libido, ie energy II

emotionality II

anxiety IIIII IIIII IIIII IIIII IIIII I

inhibition IIIII III

obsessions IIIII II

depressive attitude III

agitation III

suspiciousness concerning the
outside world III

fear IIIII IIII

conscious feeling of being
inferior III

repression and inhibition IIII

depression grading to obsessive
character III

lack of self-confidence IIIII III

constant struggle against
depression III

hypersensitiveness IIIII IIIII IIIII III

emotional waste of energy IIIII I

inner conflicts IIIII IIIII IIII

inconsistency from nervous
causes I

sexual problems IIIII I

unhappiness IIII

nervousness II

dissatisfaction I

emotional agitation II

lack of emotional satisfaction II

frustrated ambition II

idealistic aspirations II

fatigability II

sado-anal II

frustrations (multiple, ie of every
kind) II

tension I

ambivalence I

Social

timidity IIIII IIIII I

touchiness IIII

despotism IIIII I

paranoia II

irritability IIIII IIIII IIIII

changing mood II

competitive aggressiveness IIIII I

obstinate, stubborn III

tends to distrust other people IIIII I

belligerence (result of inner
conflicts etc) IIIII I

aggressive impulses IIIII III

not easy to live with
(quarrelsome) III

bitterness II

schizothymic character IIIII III

avarice IIII

lack of sociability II

anger II

defensive fighting II

imperiousness II

sadism II

protesting attitude against his own
sensibility II

difficulty in adapting II

Conclusion

Woman	Man
Although she is not intolerant she could not bear:	
Intellectually: his pedantic, narrow-minded and negative perfectionalism.	*Intellectually*: he would be envious of her quick intellect, adaptability and pragmatic ability in work.
Emotionally: his demands, resentfulness and suspicion.	*Emotionally*: he would envy her social success even though he considered her superficial and vain.

It would be she who ran away from him, not the other way round. A relationship between these two people would be almost impossible because they are opposites in serious ways. This analysis shows that similar cultural interests, although important, are far from being conclusive.

Comparison

After going through the first five stages of the chart to gathering the traits in groups, these are the conclusions.

Mental
Woman

Her intellect is in harmony with her feeling although this latter plays the leading role. The emotional aspect of her personality is counterbalanced by her natural energy.

She is imaginative, intuitive, flexible and graceful in her ability to communicate. Her mental activity is predominantly extroversive or pragmatic purposefulness, whereas the introversive side, or romantic imagination, is integrated but well controlled.

Man

His intellect, or way of thinking, is compulsive. He is obsessed with unnecessary details and his mind is consequently unproductive, because blocked by his inner conflicts. He is not able to apply his intellect to real problems, especially social relationships. Because of his compulsive pedantic thinking, he cannot see the wood for the trees.

Inner feelings
Woman

Her inner feelings create little problem. Her emotionality is balanced by self-confidence. She has natural energy and the ability to express herself and make human contacts.

Man

He is anxious, hypersensitive, crushed by inner conflict, nervous and dissatisfied because of his inferiority and frustration complexes. As a result he is inclined to be possessive and jealous.

Social

Woman

She is without any doubt a social extrovert of sanguine temperament, impulsive but well adapted to external reality, clever in human contact. Her social attitude is pragmatic.

Man

His ability in social intercourse is extremely limited. He is irritable, distrustful and always under the impression that he is the victim.

GRAPHOLOGY AND WORK

Suitability for the job

As jobs are a recent and artificial creation of civilization, human beings are not formed to fit them perfectly. Graphology, and especially the chart used in this book, can show quickly and clearly the areas of compatibility and of possible difficulty between the person and the form of work.

There is room here for only a quick indication of how the chart can be used for an employer's selection of a candidate for a job.

Job selection

A few words of caution for anyone wanting to work as a professional graphologist in job selection. Firstly, it is important to find out from the employer the full details of what the job entails. Secondly, work as closely as possible with the firm so that you understand the atmosphere, but never become their employee yourself. Finally, never reveal to the employer more about the candidate than he or she absolutely needs to know. The 'Inner feelings' column should not be revealed to the employer.

Vocational guidance

In vocational guidance both young people looking for a career and older people who are unhappy in their work but not sure where to turn can be saved from unreal self-assessment. In this case the 'inner feelings' and deep aspects of the personality are an important part of the analysis.

This subject is too large to deal with here, but even a quick look at the chart can help perceptions. For instance, if the chart is well to the right in 30–36 the person would be impatient in a clerical job. If the job includes a lot of stress some emotional stability is needed (20–28 not too far left) and flexibility (10–16R). On the whole a general study from chart to portrait is what is needed for vocational guidance.

A graphological report on a candidate for an employer follows. This is for a job with responsibility which requires knowledge and the ability to cooperate but not to be too submissive, and for such a placing the specific skills of graphology are useful. Some employers, however, consult a graphologist for secretarial jobs which depend more on the working place atmosphere and the boss's demands than on specific qualities.

A supermarket needs an engineer who will be in charge of all the equipment and installation, ie purchase, maintenance, and the best way of using the equipment. He or she will have to be acquainted with the current methods of security and sanitation.

The main requisite for the job is good technological knowledge, which is *not* within the graphologist's area of competence. What the latter can do is deal with the candidate's *mental* qualities for the job, his or her ability to organize and to prioritize problems, whether or not he or she has enough energy for the requirements of the job and is able to work consistently while coping with tension if necessary; and establish his or her *social* qualities for the job – the ability to deal with people.

The applicant, a 34-year-old man, graduated from a well-known school of engineering and has good work experience. The graphologist goes through the first five stages as usual. Here, as there is no room for the five stages the chart is commented on directly.

Referring to the graph on page 143:

0–6R + 10–16R: The applicant's mental activity can be applied to what he wants to achieve.

The crosses are all on the same side of the chart (from the middle line to RC); this shows intellectual flexibility and also commitment to reality.

In the 20–28 area: 20–23 is on the right since the lay-out is good. The applicant is able to conform when necessary.

Only 25 and 26 are moderately on the left side of the chart. This is unavoidable because of the speed (0–16R). It is a supporting sign of mental flexibility.

If we associate 0–6R and 10–16R with good lay-out (20–23R) and flexible irregularities (25–26L) the applicant's intellectual balance and sense of organization is clearly satisfactory.

In the 30–36 area: 30–36 is mainly on the left of the chart. This, combined with 0–6R, 10–16R and 20–28 balanced between left and right, shows the applicant as a reserved man who never acts on impulse but considers things carefully. Furthermore the flexible

CHART		mkd LC	mod LB	sli LA	sli RA	mod RB	mkd RC		
Emphasized first letters	0			×	•	×		0	Unemphasized first letters
Care of elaboration	1			×	•	×		1	Streamlined simplification
Left tendency: MZ	2			×	•	×		2	Right tendency: MZ
Left tending word endings	3			×	•	×		3	Right tending word endings
Left tendency: LZ	4				•			4	Right tendency: LZ
Left tendency: UZ	5					•		5	Right tendency: UZ
Interrupted movement	6			×		•	×	6	Connected movement
Narrowing or neat L margin	10				•			10	Widening L margin
Descending lines or words	11					•		11	Rising lines
Unmodulated pressure	12				•			12	Modulated pressure
Arcade connective forms	13					•		13	Garlandic connective forms
Slant stiffness	14				•			14	Slant flexibility
Close downstrokes	15					•		15	Wide-apart downstrokes
Close-packed letters	16				•			16	Wide-apart letters
Lines or words unparallel	20					•		20	Lines and words parallel
Irregular word spacing	21					•		21	Regular word spacing
Irregular margins	22				•			22	Regular margins
Irregular 'i'-dots	23				•			23	Regular 'i'-dots
Irregular slant	24				•			24	Regular slant
Irregular MZ height	25		•					25	Regular MZ height
Irregular LZ	26		•					26	Regular LZ
Disturbed pressure	27				•			27	Undisturbed pressure
Disturbed curves	28				•			28	Undisturbed curves
Lean MZ ovals	30					•		30	Full MZ ovals
Wide right margin	31			•				31	No right margin
Limited movement (any zone)	32		×	•	×			32	Animated movement (any zone)
Short LZ	33	×		•	×			33	Long LZ
Lean LZ	34		•					34	Full LZ
Clear interlines	35		•					35	Overlapping projections
Low 'i'-dots	36		•					36	High 'i'-dots
Wide space between words	40		•					40	Narrow space between words
Lines not straight	41				•			41	Lines straight
Downstroke not straight	42			•				42	Downstrokes straight
Weak pressure	43			•				43	Strong pressure
Soft or unfinished endings	44			•				44	Stress on ending strokes
Weak or omitted 't'-bars	45			•				45	Stressed 't'-bars/cross-strokes
Soft rounded forms	46		•					46	Angular forms
Inadequate spacing	50				•			50	Adequate spacing
Letters out of proportion	51					•		51	Letters in proportion
Slow from any cause (0–16L)	52				•			52	Natural and fast (0–16R)
Conventional forms	53				•			53	Individual forms
Stiffness or monotony	54				•			54	Natural rhythm

UZ = Upper zone   MZ = Middle zone   LZ = Lower zone

Hubert Desenclos Copyright © 1990

stroke movement (in the garlandic forms of 13R) and the moderate width in MZ (15R and 16R) associated with reasonably full MZ ovals (30R) show a reasonable degree of sociability and human understanding.

In the 40–46 area: In this category the candidate's chart is mainly on the centre or to the left except for 41R (firm and straight lines). This should not be taken as inability to be firm when necessary in a diplomatic way. The wide space between words (40L) should be, as always, interpreted according to the context. The applicant is reserved, cautious, but sociable (10–16R and 30R). The open right-tending terminal stroke (3R) shows that the movement between words is not interrupted. Furthermore, the regularity of these widely spaced words shows a good sense of organization. The stroke movement is soft but far from being slack and the lines are straight and slightly rising. The 46L reveals an absence of rigidity.

In the 50–54 area: The chart here is on the right side which supports what has been said about his intellectual balance and shows him as able to cope with different kinds of people, seeing problems objectively and more concerned with what has to be done than with his own prestige.

Report to employer

The report to the employer should be brief and to the point.

Mental

The applicant is methodical, analytical and accurate, but also able to criticize and to think ahead in a rational way, with a sense of reality. He is also capable of initiating new methods.

Social

He is a reserved but sociable man, adapted to rules and conventions but nevertheless with an understanding of human problems. He is diplomatic in a sincere way and can gain people's confidence.

Conclusion

The applicant is highly recommended. His tempo is poised and consistent, with the ability to withstand stress. His actions and initiatives are well balanced because of his ability to prioritize problems.

NB   It should be noticed that all points of this report are part of the applicant's observable behaviour and will be obvious to the employer during the first three months of employment.